Siebold and Japan

His life and work

Arlette Kouwenhoven

Matthi Forrer

 Hotei Publishing, Leiden

Colophon

Publisher

Hotei Publishing

Zoeterwoudsesingel 56

2313 EK Leiden

The Netherlands

www.hotei-publishing.com

Copyright

© 2000, Hotei Publishing, Arlette
Kouwenhoven and Matthi Forrer

ISBN 90-74822-19-3

NUGI 646

ISBN 90-74822-27-4 (Dutch)

ISBN 90-74822-33-9 (Japanese)

Text

Arlette Kouwenhoven and Matthi Forrer

Translation

Mark Poysden

Design

Robert Schaap, Bergeijk

Printing

Snoeck-Ducaju & Zoon, Ghent, Belgium

Photography

Ben Grishaaver, AVC, National Museum of
Ethnology (RMV, Leiden)

Ben Kieft, National Herbarium, Leiden

Carla Teune, Hortus Botanicus, Leiden

Carol Winkel, Amsterdam

Cover illustration

Philipp Franz von Siebold, lithograph by
E. Chiossone, 1875

Background: The Sieboldhuis on the
Rapenburg in the year 2000.

Contents

1. Philipp Franz von Siebold,
lithograph by E. Chiossone, 1875

Foreword

Four centuries ago this year (2000), the frigate *De Liefde* was the first Dutch ship to dock in Japan. Following the expulsion of the Portuguese in 1639, Holland would be the only Western nation to conduct a trading relationship with Japan, which otherwise remained closed to the rest of the world until 1854.

The year 2000 marks the anniversary of this exclusive relationship between Japan and Holland, and the newly established museum, the Sieboldhuis, will be opened on 4 April 2000 to celebrate this event. It is situated at 19 Rapenburg, which is the house where Philipp Franz von Siebold based himself from 1832 to 1840. It was here that he first publicly exhibited his collection of natural historical and ethnographic objects that he had brought with him from Japan. Now, a century and a half later, part of Siebold's collections will again be exhibited to the public in the same house, from April to October. The Sieboldhuis will be permanently open to the public in the spring of 2002, after some major renovations have occurred.

This book about Philipp Franz von Siebold has been written to mark this occasion. It is in no way intended to be a complete record of his activities; it endeavours instead to provide an impression of the life and work of a man whose love for Japan had an important influence on the development of Western sciences in Japan, as well as on Western knowledge of that nation.

We are very grateful to the following people for the assistance they provided: Constantin von Brandenstein-Zeppelin, Jeanette Ridder-Numan and Ingrid de Kort of the National Herbarium, Leiden University Branche, Carla Teune of the Hortus Botanicus in Leiden, Mark Nozeman of the National Museum of Ethnology in Leiden, the Municipal Archives in Leiden and the Netherlands Maritime Museum in Amsterdam, all of whom assisted in obtaining photographic material. Ben Grishaaver and Carol Winkel took many of the photographs included in this book. We also wish to express our appreciation to Max Put, who generously provided valuable advice on the manuscript.

2. Porcelain serving tray for sweets, with handle and decorated with an ivy motif. (National Museum of Ethnology, Leiden).

Introduction

I arrived safely in Japan and am spending the happiest days of my life working in the fields of natural history and medical science. In this way, I learn about one of the most interesting countries in the world. Over the next few years, I intend to write a number of dissertations on the current state of medicine, surgery and obstetrics in Japan. [...] I have written an essay about the natural history of Japan and have described twenty-five animal species, which have not yet been classified as indigenous in any writings about Japan. I have also made many zoological and even more botanical discoveries. Every week I give lectures, in Dutch, on both medicine and natural sciences. I do not intend to leave Japan until I have described it in detail and until I have collected enough material for a Japanese museum and a flora. [1]

This quotation from a letter sent on 18 November 1823 by Philipp Franz von Siebold to his uncle, Adam Elias von Siebold (1775-1828), a mere three months after his arrival on Deshima testifies to the character, intentions and passion of this enthusiastic physician and researcher.[2] The Dutch government had appointed Siebold to the post of Surgeon-Major of the hospitals and troops in the Dutch East Indies. A few months after this the Governor-General of the Dutch East Indies sent him to Japan, where he was to work as the physician at the trading post on Deshima. He was also commissioned to conduct research into the laws and constitution of Japan. Siebold performed these tasks meticulously and with great pride. As a physician, he introduced the principles of Western diagnostics to Japan, in itself no small achievement. He also became famous because of his cataract operations, a completely unknown surgical procedure in Japan at that time. He introduced a number of Western medical techniques, especially in the fields of obstetrics and anaesthesia, and treated innumerable people for both major and minor ailments. His proclivity to help people and to share his knowledge of Western sciences was met with an enormous response, not least because Siebold displayed such a keen interest in Japan and its people. His task was to gather as much information as he could about Japan, its inhabitants and the indigenous flora and fauna, be it as texts, illustrations or as actual samples and objects. He was greatly assisted in this by the large number of patients, students and friends with whom he had become acquainted with during his six-year stay on Deshima. His passion and occasionally foolhardy desire to fulfil his mission eventually landed him in deep trouble. He was suspected of being engaged in espionage, and although he narrowly escaped being sentenced to death, was banned from Japan for life. The purpose of this book is to provide an insight into Siebold as a person and a scientist. He was a man who is praised by most authors for his talents and achievements, but whose egoism was often an obstacle to the fulfilment of his ambitions.

3. Otaria stelleri, *taken from* the Fauna Japonica.

His early years in Germany

'I wish to end this letter by once again repeating my promise to honour the name Von Siebold and, with God's blessing, to uphold its reputation in Würzburg.' Siebold was studying medicine at the University of Würzburg, also the city where he was born in 1796, when he wrote these lines to his Uncle Elias in 1818. He had been lodging for a year-and-a-half with Ignaz Döllinger (1770-1841), the Professor of Anatomy and Physiology. Döllinger had been giving him daily guidance in his studies of anatomy, botany and physics and Siebold considered him his patron. Döllinger's house was a meeting place for scholars from a broad spectrum of disciplines, and Siebold's pervasive interest in science undoubtedly flourished here. Ignaz Döllinger was an old university friend of Siebold's father, Johann Georg Christoph von Siebold (1767-1798), who died when Phillip was only two years old. His father had been a Professor of Medicine and Surgery, and his grandfather Karl Kaspar von Siebold (1736-1807) was one of the most famous physicians of his time. Small wonder then that Philipp Franz von Siebold had pledged to uphold his family name. He was to spend five years studying before finally receiving his doctorate, after which he worked for two-and-a-half years as a medical surgeon and obstetrician in Heijdingsfeld, the city where his mother Apollonia von Siebold-Lotz (1768-1845) settled after the death of her husband. It was at this point that his life was to take a dramatic turn.

In the service of the Dutch Government

Siebold had decided early in his career that he wanted to conduct scientific research in distant countries. He originally thought of going to Brazil and

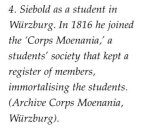

4. Siebold as a student in Würzburg. In 1816 he joined the 'Corps Moenania,' a students' society that kept a register of members, immortalising the students. (Archive Corps Moenania, Würzburg).

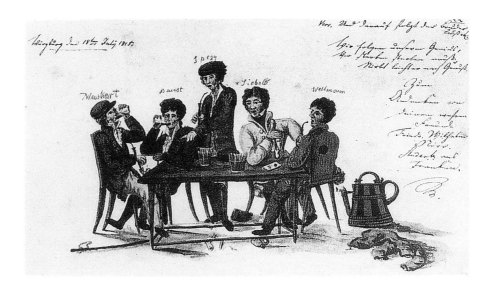

became a member of the Senckenberg Natural History Society in Frankfurt, who gave him the task of acquiring a collection of natural historical objects for the recently established museum there. However, intervention by Franz Harbaur, a friend of the family who worked for the Dutch Health Service, resulted in him being offered the opportunity of applying for the post of Military Physician in the service of the Dutch government. He would be based in the Dutch East Indies. He was accepted and appointed Surgeon-Major in June 1822. Siebold considered that working in this capacity for the Dutch army was the ideal job for him, and he wrote in a letter to a friend:

> *My love of natural history and research developed in my early youth and flourished under the guidance of my eternally beloved tutor, Döllinger. This predilection convinced me to risk taking a great step and travel to another, very remote part of the world. No doubt it will also be the basis of all the useful results that will arise from this journey.*[3]

Siebold embarked on the *Jonge Adriana* in Rotterdam on 23 September 1822, which arrived in Batavia five months later. He began his research while on board the ship, collecting marine animals and making notes to help pass the time. His duties as the ship's doctor also kept him busy. At least 52 of the 100 soldiers, 33 male passengers and the few women and children who were making the voyage fell sick during the trip, but Siebold managed to cure them.

5. Johann Georg Christoph von Siebold (1767-1798). (Municipal Archives, Leiden).

6. Apollonia von Siebold-Lotz (1768-1845). (Municipal Archives, Leiden).

His first trip to Japan

His sojourn in Java was to be a short one. The resident Governor-General of the Dutch East Indies, Godert Baron van der Capellen (1778-1848) was greatly impressed with his abilities, and a few months after Siebold arrived in Java, suggested that he join the new Dutch delegation to Japan, and be appointed to the post of Surgeon-Physician at the trading post on Deshima. He was primarily motivated by the fact that he considered Siebold an inspired researcher, who would undoubtedly immerse himself in the geography, the political system, the local customs, and the flora and fauna of this largely unknown country, much like his contemporary, Professor Caspar Reinwardt (1773-1854) had done in the Dutch East Indies during the years 1816 to 1822. He was also ordered to accumulate a fine collection. This was not only a politically motivated decision, as Van der Capellen was certain that this research would be a significant step towards understanding the people and culture of a country that Holland had an exclusive trading relationship with. Japan had always had a great admiration for Western science and an envoy like Siebold would not only be very welcome, but also highly beneficial to the trade relations between the two countries. Even Colonel De Sturler (1777-1855), the imminent *Opperhoofd*, or Chief of the trading post on Deshima, intended to put the young doctor to work treating Japanese patients and teaching Western medical techniques to Japanese physicians as a gesture of appreciation for the goodwill that the Japanese had displayed to the Dutch for the preceding two centuries. Japan had displayed an interest in Western medicine since the middle of the 18th century, as can be deduced from the fact that a study *Kaitai shinsho* ('A new book on anatomy'), based on *Ontleedkundige tafelen* by Johan Adam Kulmus (1689-1745), had been published in Japan in 1774. This book is generally considered to mark the beginning of the *Rangaku*, or the 'Dutch sciences' in Japan. The Dutch had already caused a sensation early in the 18th century, when they had taken some of their scientific instruments on a court journey and presented them to the shogun. There are books dating from the 1730s and 1740s, which depict demonstrations of an electrostatic generator. Siebold also made the appropriate preparations and took along an electrostatic generator, an air pump and a galvanising apparatus, with the intention of arousing the interest of the Japanese and making them more amenable to exchanging information with him. He had a budget of 1827 guilders, which he could use to purchase all the necessary materials and equipment in Batavia that he might require on his journey to, and during his stay in Japan. These

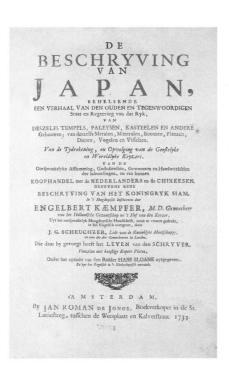

7. De beschryving van Japan *by Kaempfer, 1733 (original Dutch ed. 1729; English ed.* The history of Japan, *1727); one of the works that formed the basis of Siebold's knowledge of Japan.*

39. *Title-page from the book by Kaempfer.*

were not limited to medical instruments, pharmaceutical equipment and therapeutic apparatus for his own use, but also included wine, beer and other commercial items. 'One almost has to be a merchant,' complained Siebold. He took all the literature on Japan that he could find including the work of Montanus (1669), the flora (1712) and *The history of Japan* (1727) by the former doctor at the trading post, Engelbert Kaempfer (1651-1716). He also took the *Flora Japonica* (1784) by Carl Peter Thunberg (1743-1828), a Swedish professor who had also been a doctor at the trading post. Thunberg had studied under Carl von Linné (Linnaeus) (1707-1778), who had introduced the Linnaean system of plant classification – as explained in his *Systema natura* of 1735 – to Japan. Siebold later expressed his amazement at the fact that the Japanese were already familiar with this system.

The ship *De Drie Gezusters* departed from Batavia on 23 June and, after what seemed like a successful start, sailed into a severe typhoon off the coast of Taiwan. They were at least five days journey from Nagasaki when they saved a few unfortunate castaways whose own vessel had been wrecked by the storm. 'They were the first Japanese people that we saw and their competence and refined behaviour was most astonishing,' wrote Siebold. He was immediately captivated by Nagasaki, with its beautiful bays and surrounding hills covered with small white houses and temples. The castaways were met by their colleagues, who gave their day's catch to the Dutch to express their gratitude. In this way, Siebold's first impressions of the Japanese had already been positively influenced, even before he actually set foot on the shore of the country to which he would willingly dedicate the rest of his life.

Deshima

Before the arrival in 1543 of the Portuguese, who were the first Europeans to reach Japan, the country was embroiled in a period of civil wars which lasted until the end of the 16th century. The Emperors had little authority and the country was divided into territories ruled by feudal overlords, who were constantly at war with each other. Even Buddhist sects terrorised their neighbouring areas. The Portuguese brought firearms with them and these hastened the rise to power of Oda Nobunaga (1534-1582), who hoped to unify the country. His successor, Toyotomi Hideyoshi (1536-1598) almost managed to do this, but it was Tokugawa Ieyasu (1542-1616) who eventually succeeded in establishing the lasting dynasty of Tokugawa-shoguns who ruled the country until the Meiji Restoration of 1868.

When the Portuguese arrived in Nagasaki in 1570, it was still a small village surviving off its agriculture and fishing. They recognised the potential of this beautiful natural harbour, which presented an ideal anchorage for their merchant ships, and obtained permission to establish a trading post. Before long, Nagasaki blossomed into a lively, flourishing town with merchants' houses, where both the Japanese and the Portuguese lived. However this

9. View of Deshima and the harbour in Nagasaki, after Keiga, taken from Nippon.

situation was not to last; one of the reasons was that the Portuguese Jesuits were so successful in their efforts to convert the Japanese to Christianity. At one point, the Japanese Christian community consisted of as many as 300,000 people. The church started to meddle in all sorts of internal affairs, including politics, and the shoguns soon realised that Catholicism presented an increasingly dangerous threat to the unification of Japan. Tokugawa Iemitsu, the shogun who ruled the country from 1622-1651, finally persecuted the Christians most severely. The Jesuits were banished and the influence of their compatriots was reduced to a minimum. As it was still desirable to maintain the trading activities, Iemitsu ordered the excavation of one of the hills on the Bay of Nagasaki so that the ground could be used to construct the artificial island of Deshima. This name is derived from the Japanese words *deru* – go out, and *shima* – island, freely translated as 'the island that lies in front of the city'. The Portuguese were restricted to conducting their trading activities from here. A large rebellion broke out at Shimabara in 1637/38 and many Christians supported the local farmers' resistance to the way the country was being mismanaged. This was the final straw, and the Portuguese were ordered to leave the island, and Japan itself. The Dutch, who had already been operating from the trading post in Hirado for a number of decades, had restrained from any form of Christian practise and could now replace the Portuguese on Deshima. The Chinese were also allowed to trade with Japan from an island not far from Deshima. In this way the Dutch were the only European nation permitted to trade with a country that would otherwise remain virtually isolated from the rest of the world until 1854. This trade centred around exports of gold, silver and copper, and the Dutch supplied cotton from Holland, Chinese silk, Indian spices, raw materials like gum, lead, tin, elephant ivory, leather, skins, tropical wood and rare Dutch items like spectacles, mirrors, clocks and glassware. However, the Japanese decided to keep their precious metals for their own domestic market and Dutch trade was never what it had been in the early years. In 1638, twelve ships were allowed to dock at Deshima; after 1641 this was reduced to six or seven and after 1715 only one or two ships were permitted to land each year. Trade with Japan had all but collapsed in the years just before Siebold's arrival on Deshima, and this was partly due to the political changes in Europe at the time. The United East India Company, or VOC *(Vereenigde Nederlandse Oost-Indische Compagnie)* had been declared bankrupt in 1798, and the Batavian Republic had assumed all its debts and liabilities, which meant that Deshima fell under the direct control of the Governor-General and the Council of the Dutch East Indies. Napoleon had invaded the Batavian Republic in 1806; and in 1811, England took advantage of the prevailing situation in Europe and occupied the Dutch East Indies (and other Dutch settlements in South East Asia) for a while. It was eventually returned in 1816 to the Kingdom of the Netherlands, which had declared its sovereignty in 1813. This turmoil meant

10. Deshima. Illustration from Souvenir du Japon, *Van Lijnden, 1860.*

that the Dutch on Deshima had no contact with Holland from 1807 to 1817. The desire for international trade soon returned after this turbulent period, leading to the establishment of the Netherlands Trading Company *(Nederlandse Handelmaatschappij)* in 1824. Deshima remained an unprofitable trading post, but the government maintained it more for political than economic reasons, as it was prudent to continue to acquire information about trading partners in a rapidly changing political arena. Earlier, the English Governor Thomas Stamford Raffles (1781-1826), who had been posted in Batavia from 1811-1816, had researched the history, the natural history and the culture of the Indies, which had provided a great deal of valuable information about that country. Similarly, such knowledge about Japan would be just as important. Indeed, when Siebold wrote his book *Nippon*, he was to use Raffles's *The history of Java* (2 vols. 1817) as his model.

The fan-shaped island of Deshima was not more than 65 metres deep, 175 metres wide on the side facing the city and 215 metres wide on the side facing the sea, and it was surrounded by a basalt wall. The island had two gateways, one on the west side, called the 'Water Gate' *(Waterpoort)* where Dutch ships docked and offloaded, and another main gate that connected the island to the city of Nagasaki on the mainland. Both entrances were heavily guarded. Only the captains of the ships were allowed to enter Deshima; sailors had to remain on board. Those who wished to enter or leave Deshima, even temporarily, were subject to a thorough inspection and body search at the gateways, which was supposed to discourage smuggling, a proliferate problem. These checks were performed twice so that the Japanese could control each other. These inspectors and scrutineers were not very popular and many Dutchmen were daunted by this unpleasant prospect which awaited them when they arrived on Deshima. As Captain Van Assendelft de Coningh (1821-1890), who visited Japan in 1845 and 1851 was to observe later:

I was filled with fear after I had managed to escape from the clutches of the inspectors and entered Deshima through the two solemn gateways where the guards were sitting on mats like silent mummies. The high walls, which enclosed the island, gave me the feeling that we were criminals who had been imprisoned in some sort of institution.[4]

According to De Coningh, the *Opperhoofds* were exempt from such scrutiny, which meant that 'many disembarked on the island as corpulent men and re-emerged from their houses a few minutes later as thin as rakes.'
A sign, which had been placed at the main entrance to the island, bore an equally plain message: no women (with the exception of prostitutes), priests or beggars were allowed to set foot on Deshima and the Dutch were only allowed to leave it with a permit. Being in possession of a bible was also outlawed so as to avert any possible Christian influences, and these had to be placed in a special repository, the 'bible-barrel' before entering Deshima. This actually happened for a while, but soon the barrels were filled with hay and stones and according to De Coningh, bibles were successfully smuggled ashore, although he was cautious enough to tear out the title page first. The Japanese were not so naïve as to be unaware of these sorts of practises, but cast a blind eye on them when it became apparent that the Dutch were not particularly pious anyway. Engelbert Kaempfer, a German physician employed by the Dutch, who was stationed on Deshima at the end of the 17th century, apparently soon tired of the restrictions imposed by the Japanese, and wrote:

The Dutch were so greedy, and the attraction of the Japanese gold so irresistible, that rather than relinquish the prospects of a truly beneficial trade, they willingly submitted to what was virtually lifelong imprisonment – because that is what our existence on Deshima actually amounted to. They had chosen instead to sustain much privation in a strange and heathen country, to disregard their religious duties on Sundays and holidays, to neglect their prayers and singing psalms, making the sign of the cross, invoking God's name and to not refer to their Christian beliefs while in the presence of the indigenous population. Moreover, what can be more insulting to men of noble and excellent heart than to have to patiently and humbly accept the coarse and offensive behaviour of such proud unbelievers![5]

Siebold's arrival

This was the prevailing climate that awaited Siebold when he arrived in Nagasaki on 23 August 1823. As usual, Japanese officials and interpreters boarded the ship to check the cargo and crew. Siebold was nearly refused entry to the country when the Japanese interpreters realised that they spoke better Dutch than he did and asked him if he really was from The Netherlands. Their ignorance of geographical specifics worked in his favour when he answered the he was a 'High German' *(Hoogduitser)*, which was subsequently translated by the Japanese as *Yama-Orandajin*, or 'Dutchman from the mountains'.[6]

There were eleven houses at the disposal of the Dutch officials, which doubled up as warehouses; the living quarters were always located on the first floor. In addition there were a number of buildings which were also used as warehouses, kitchens, a sick-bay, cow stalls and pig sties, (guard) houses for the Japanese staff and such-like. Siebold moved into the building that served as the doctors' quarters. The house was fitted with all Western conveniences. Siebold had brought a piano with him, which he played frequently.

There were probably twelve, certainly not more than fifteen Dutchmen on Deshima, with a couple of Malaysian servants. Ship's captains were only present during the trading season, which occurred from July/August until November/December. It took Siebold some time to get used to the Dutchmen who were already living on Deshima, as he wrote later:

Initially, we did not have a pleasant impression of the formal court behaviour these men adopted towards each other, and to the Japanese officials, nor of the old-fashioned clothing which they wore [...], which consisted of quilted velvet coats and black cloaks, hats with feathers, steel swords and Spanish canes with gold handles [...]. However, after a few days we got accustomed to this way of associating with the Japanese officials and the Dutch representatives at the trading post, and with the prevailing atmosphere on Deshima. It felt as though we were taking part in a 17th century ceremony [...].[7]

Siebold could not fault this behaviour considering the length of time these men had been isolated from their own country and the limited resources they had at their disposal, and it did not take him long to settle down. He was on an annual wage of 5000 guilders and had the freedom to supplement his lifestyle with various forms of trade. Three months after his arrival he wrote the often quoted observation to his uncle Elias, 'Everything is to my great satisfaction here on my small island, Deshima. I live in domestic bliss, and this, together with ceaseless activity as far as my scientific and medical pursuits are concerned, ensures that these must surely be the happiest days of my life.'

His work as a physician and teacher

The few Dutchmen at the trading post who required his medical services were hardly enough to fill his time. In order to conduct his scientific research more efficiently, he also established relationships with Japanese doctors and scholars, who were used to being taught by the Dutch physicians. This was a tactic his famous predecessors Thunberg and Kaempfer had also used, and it had to happen in secret as only prostitutes and interpreters were allowed to visit the island. The doctors managed to pass through the gate by pretending to be the interpreters' assistants, which meant that sometimes there were up to fifty interpreters for just a handful of Dutchmen. This did not escape the attention of the Governor of Nagasaki, who eventually ensured that these doctors were granted permission to visit Deshima to further their education. Soon Siebold's house was filled with scientists who were tutored in a variety of disciplines in the Dutch language, or 'The Latin of the East' as it was called then. Siebold was also granted extra privileges and he was allowed to leave

11. Narutaki, where Siebold established the first school in Japan that taught Western medicine.
(Municipal Archives, Leiden).

Siebold's medical practise

Siebold's activities as a doctor were highly prized in Japan, if the long queues of people who waited to benefit from his treatments could be taken as an indication, but it remains unclear how successful he was as a doctor by Western standards. He was sent to the Far East a mere two years after he qualified, so he could hardly have had much practical experience. On the other hand, he did study at Würzburg, the centre of European medicine at that time. Whatever the case, it is certain that the standard of Japanese surgical techniques, obstetrics and ophthalmology, was not particularly high, so Siebold stood out from his Japanese colleagues. His merits lay mostly in his work as a teacher and in how he continued to disseminate knowledge of Western medicine in Japan. He propagated a system of 'practical learning,' in which his pupils learnt primarily from hands-on experience. For instance, he taught them all sorts of surgical techniques at his clinic in Narutaki. He made definite contributions in those areas that interested him most, namely ophthalmology and obstetrics, and he successfully stimulated the use of surgical forceps as an aid in difficult deliveries. Forceps were already known in Japan, but a lack of knowledge meant that they were rarely used. Siebold was extremely interested in Japanese obstetrics, and he explained the then contemporary methods of the Kagawa School in a paper titled: *Answers to some questions concerning Japanese obstetrics by my student Mimazunzo [Mima Junzō], a doctor at Nagasaki; presented to The Batavian Society of Arts and Sciences by the Medical Doctor Siebold (1825).*[8] This document is a record of the information the two doctors exchanged on how to diagnose pregnancy, how children were delivered, and which remedies were used during the procedure, especially in the case of an induced birth. The absence of the practical use of surgical forceps became clear to Siebold when he asked: 'When a child has only partially appeared, for example with only a hand, an arm or a foot showing, and it cannot be brought into the world, then what procedure does the obstetrician recommend?' The answer was that firstly they attempted to assist the birth using their hands and fingers to avoid causing any harm to the child, but, when necessary, 'one also uses a knife or a hook to cut the child into pieces or scrape it out of the womb in those cases where the child has already

died in its mother's body; or has extremely fat buttocks, which makes it impossible for it to be born in a natural way.' The Japanese never resorted to using the Caesarean section: already a common technique in Europe, 'no matter how aware they are that the Caesarean section or cutting the abdomen is the only course of action to take. It can be attributed to their fear, or rather their abhorrence of this procedure, and common folk would rather see the unfortunate patient die than that this major, but frightening and dangerous operation be performed.'
It is often stated that Siebold introduced the cowpox vaccine to Japan but this is based on a misunderstanding. Doeff and Blomhoff, who had both been *Opperhoofds* on Deshima before Siebold's arrival, had already had the vaccine sent to them from Batavia when similar epidemics had broken out in Japan, but it was ineffective when it arrived. The same thing happened to Siebold, and it was only introduced successfully some time later. Siebold had considerably less experience in ophthalmics in comparison to his well-known Japanese colleagues, including the physician Habu Genseki. It is said that on one occasion Siebold asked for a pig's head to be brought to him so that he could first practise a complicated eye operation on it, before actually operating on his patient. On the other hand, Siebold provided Genseki with atropine, a particularly valuable preparation that was used to dilate the pupil of the eye, enabling eye surgery to be performed more easily. Genseki considered it such an important substance that he gave Siebold a tabard with the Imperial emblem on it in exchange for it: a deed for which he was later to be punished.

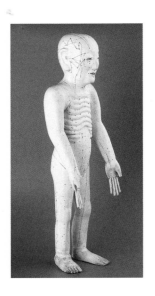

12. Acupuncture doll. (National Museum of Ethnology, Leiden).

13. Lacquered box with acupuncture needles. (National Museum of Ethnology, Leiden).

Siebold, in his turn, introduced a number of Japanese medical procedures to the West, including *moxa* techniques. The use of *moxa* in the Far East was already known in Europe, but Siebold considered the Japanese method the superior one. However, Siebold was primarily occupied with acupuncture. He had a translation made of a dissertation by the Imperial Acupuncturist, Ishizaka Sotetsu, which he published in 1833 in the *Transactions of the Batavian Society of Arts and Sciences*. Siebold practised the technique on chicks, as well as on himself, and discovered that it was a relatively painless treatment.

Siebold would only practise medicine in Japan, however. After his return to Europe, he devoted himself to processing his information, organising his collections and cultivating plants. He did offer his assistance during the cholera epidemic of 1832, as he had acquired much experience with this disease in Japan, but as he had alternative ideas on the correct way of treating it, his help was not accepted.

14. An arm being amputated; Japanese woodblock print. (Kobe City Museum, Japan).

15. Lobster in formalin. (National Museum of Ethnology, Leiden).

the island to attend to Japanese patients and look for herbs in the vicinity of Nagasaki.

There was a steady increase in the number of students who attended his lessons, and the results of his diagnoses and treatments were noticed more and more. Siebold received permission to establish a medical school in Nagasaki in 1824. A group of his students negotiated on his behalf and Siebold, using a false Japanese name, was able to buy a small plot of approximately two hectares in the Narutaki ('The Murmuring Waterfall') Valley.

In time, two large buildings and three smaller ones were constructed, and it was here that Siebold started his school, called *Narutaki juku*, where he held lectures once a week for those students who were not permitted to visit Deshima. It was the first school in Japan that taught Western medicine. Lessons were taught in Dutch and consisted of theoretical and practical medicine, natural history and pharmacology.

His book *Materia medica*, a concise dissertation on remedies in which he discussed one hundred therapeutic herbs used in Western medicine, was written during this period. Thirty-five of these herbs also grew in Japan, and his book was translated into Japanese by one of his students and many copies were eventually distributed throughout the country.

A botanical garden was planted around the house and these, and other local medicinal plants were cultivated there. Siebold was also asked by the Governor of Batavia to establish a botanical garden on a plot of land next to his house on Deshima. He lived on the ground floor of his house in Narutaki and used the first floor as a storage space for his rapidly expanding collection of curiosities, including numerous jars with preserved animal specimens. People suffering from a wide variety of complaints visited his clinic in Narutaki, and Siebold performed many operations, which his students were allowed to observe. He was extremely satisfied, as he later wrote in *Nippon*, 'A new ray of scientific illumination beams out across Japan from the Atheneum we established here, and with it a sign of our solidarity with this nation.' However, it was the cataract operations he performed, which restored sight to practically blind patients that earned him the sobriquet 'Miracle Doctor'. This recognition enabled Siebold to make use of the best available possibilities at his disposal to further his already successful scientific work.

Siebold's Japanese 'wife'

Siebold made regular house-calls to his Japanese patients. During one of these visits, probably in the winter of 1823, the twenty-seven year old doctor met a sixteen-year old girl called Kusumoto Otaki (1807-1865), who also went by the name Sonogi. The pair fell in love but it was not possible at the time for a

Oine

Siebold and Sonogi had a daughter called Oine who, like every Dutch father of a Japanese child, he had to leave behind when he left Japan. Oine was more than two years old at the time. Siebold asked his two most trusted students, Kō Ryōsai and Ninomiya Keisaku, to share the task of raising his daughter. When Oine was nineteen years old, and was called Ine, her mother gave her permission to go and lodge with Ninomiya, who had a medical practise in Iyo Province. Ninomiya was keen to teach this inquisitive girl, and advised her to specialise in obstetrics. She later studied with a variety of masters, and had a child by one of them, before eventually returning to Ninomiya and working with him. They moved back to Nagasaki when her father returned to Japan for the first time in thirty years, after his banishment was revoked. Ine wanted to be close to him, and learn from him too. The three of them had intensive contact regarding the treatment of their patients, and Siebold supplied his daughter with Western medicines. Ine became Japan's first female doctor/obstetrician and would practise in a number of places. She was appointed to the post of Imperial Obstetrician in 1877. She died in 1903, aged seventy-six.

16. Otaksa, also called Sonogi. Siebold's great Japanese love, taken from Nippon.

OTAKSA.

Dutchman to marry a Japanese woman. The Dutch men on Deshima were expected to find satisfaction in the company of the prostitutes who were allowed to visit the island. It is not known where Sonogi came from; according to some sources she was a prostitute, and as such was allowed to consort with Siebold, while others maintain that she loved him so much that she willingly allowed a red courtesan stamp to be placed in her passport. Sonogi might well have been her courtesan name. Siebold was very happy with her and wrote to his uncle Lotz, 'I have given in to that old Dutch habit and have temporarily become quite attached to a sweet sixteen-year old Japanese girl, who I would not willingly exchange for a European one.'

Sonogi lived with him in his house and on 10 May 1827, gave birth to a daughter who they named Oine. Siebold assisted in the birth, which occurred in the operating room on Deshima. This was in itself a remarkable event because none of the prostitutes, who had many times before conceived children with the Dutch men living there, were allowed to give birth on Deshima. Besides, children were not allowed on Deshima and following the birth of their daughter, Sonogi was obliged to move with their child to Nagasaki. Siebold saw them frequently, visiting them in the morning and at night and ensured that they did not lack a thing. Sonogi was devoted to him, and was his staunch supporter even during those difficult times when he had been accused of espionage and was subject to gruelling cross-examinations.

Bringing together the collections

The Japanese were forbidden from selling, or making gifts of material or books with a historical, political or geographical content. This list also included any objects of a religious, strategic or ritual nature, even if they were only toys. This obviously complicated Siebold's task of collecting any material connected to these subjects, so he had to resort to the method employed by his predecessors, Thunberg, Kaempfer and Isaac Titsingh (1745-1812). He asked his students to write dissertations on medicine, physics, the country, its history, its people, their customs and the legal system. The students were awarded their doctor's diplomas based on these dissertations, although they often had no connection whatsoever to medical matters. They were written in Dutch, which meant that they could not be directly understood by all the supervisors, a few of whom were undoubtedly aware of what was going on, but were prepared to turn a blind eye in return for a gift of some sort or another. Bribery was common and Siebold must certainly have resorted to it to achieve his goals.

Knowledge of his medical prowess was soon widespread. For instance, if his arrival in a village was announced before he got there when he accompanied a

17. Bamboo basket with lid.
(National Museum of
Ethnology, Leiden).

18. A cabinet made from
woven bamboo, also depicted
in Nippon.
(National Museum of
Ethnology, Leiden).

18a. Page from Nippon.
(National Museum of
Ethnology, Leiden).

*19. Picnic set made of
lacquerwork and marquetry.
(National Museum of
Ethnology, Leiden).*

20. Sake-cup made of Hirado-porcelain with cherry blossom. (National Museum of Ethnology, Leiden).

21. Probably a sake-pitcher. Hirado-porcelain. (National Museum of Ethnology, Leiden).

court journey, the inhabitants lined the road waiting to ask him for help. Interpreters assisted in these consultations and patients were asked about their ailments and then given advice. Occasionally, misunderstandings arose because the interpreters did not always understand what Siebold meant, and so they provided some patients with information they thought up themselves. Siebold did not discriminate between the people he advised, and helped everybody regardless of their status. The only thing he asked in return for his services was that people brought him objects for his collection, and he soon accumulated a diversity of animal species, all sorts of raw materials and some unique lacquered objects. He cured an influential Japanese man, who rewarded him with a large collection of natural historical and ethnographic objects. He acquired a huge collection of objects in this way, which he stored on the first floor of his house. It consisted mainly of plants and herbs, which he attempted to seed so that he could cultivate them himself. He also had specimens of fish, birds, insects, reptiles and mammals, mostly from Osaka, which were either stuffed or preserved, and he had started acquiring books and coins immediately upon his arrival, like any true 18th century collector. After all, a good library and an extensive scientific collection were essential to his work. It was only later, during the court journey to Edo, that he started collecting ethnographic objects, or artificialia, which made his collection much more comprehensive. However, it is likely that grateful patients or students had already started presenting him with such objects before this, and no doubt these ended up in his collection too.

Siebold also started corresponding with influential people in Edo and Kyoto in an effort to expand his horizons. He made a great impression on the Japanese, who considered him different from many of his countrymen because of his intelligence and erudition. He studied both day and night and was determined to learn Japanese as quickly as possible, and to memorise the *iroha* (a poem that aided in the recollection of the Japanese syllabary), copies of which hung on every wall in his house, including in the toilet.

In 1823, Siebold wrote a letter to the Governor of Batavia requesting a draughtsman, a physicist/geologist and a medical doctor. The latter was needed to free him of his medical responsibilities, allowing him to dedicate himself fully to his scientific research. This letter was sent, together with an essay to the Minister of the Colonies, who in his turn asked the former *Opperhoofd* Hendrik Doeff (1777-1835), for his opinion on the matter. Doeff thought Siebold was pushing his luck with his request for a doctor; after all, Thunberg had never relinquished his medical duties. Two men were finally dispatched in 1825: Dr. Heinrich Bürger (1804-1858), a scholar, who worked as a pharmacist in Batavia, and who was to assist with scientific research, chemistry and mineralogy; and Carel Hubert de Villeneuve (? - after 1859),

22. Picture postcard honouring Siebold and depicting the memorial plaque for Kaempfer (incorrectly spelt on the picture) and Thunberg that Siebold erected in the garden on Deshima. The Latin text reads: 'Look! Your plants thrive and flower here and each year they produce precious flowers in memory of their protectors.' (Municipal Archives, Leiden)

Auditor, 2nd grade in the general accounts department in Batavia, who was to make the drawings.

That same year, Siebold erected a memorial to Thunberg and Kaempfer in his botanical garden on Deshima to commemorate their services to science: they had documented almost two-thirds of the flora in Japan. One of Siebold's personal achievements in the botanical field was to successfully transfer tea cultivation to Java. Governor-General Van der Capellen had previously attempted to germinate seeds on Java in 1820, but without success as the seeds dried out and lost their germinative power on the long sea voyage. Siebold packed the seeds in iron-rich loam, which apparently worked, as there were 3000 healthy tea plants growing on Java in 1827. This number had risen to half-a-million by 1833.

23. Apothecary jar with Hakusen tea. (National Museum of Ethnology, Leiden).

24. *Portrait of a Korean with Caucasian features, probably drawn by De Villeneuve. (Constantin von Brandenstein-Zeppelin, Schlüchtern, Germany).*

26. *Portrait of a Japanese boy, age 12, by De Villeneuve. (Constantin von Brandenstein-Zeppelin, Schlüchtern, Germany).*

25. Babasan, *Japanese for 'granny', drawn by De Villeneuve. (Constantin von Brandenstein-Zeppelin, Schlüchtern, Germany).*

The court journey to Edo

It did not take long for Siebold's botanical collection to become quite large and he had more than 1000 different plant varieties growing in his garden on Deshima by October 1825. However, he only really started seriously collecting ethnographic materials in 1826, the same year he was allowed to accompany the court journey to Edo.

Like the *daimyō* the *Opperhoofd* was obliged to make an annual trip to Edo almost since the beginning of the Dutch interaction with Japan.[9] The purpose of these journeys was to pay homage to the shogun as well as to personally deliver a report on their activities at the trading post. It was also a good opportunity to brush up on their knowledge of the rules governing their behaviour and trading activities. After 1790, they only undertook this journey once every four years. The return trip from Nagasaki to Edo and back again measured approximately 2800 kilometres, and it was the only opportunity they had of seeing more of Japan.

Siebold accompanied the court journey of *Opperhoofd* Johan Willem de Sturler (1777 - 1855) that departed on 15 February 1826 and was joined by Dr. Bürger, in the role of secretary, although the true purpose of him joining them was to assist Siebold in his scientific research. As only three Dutchmen were allowed to make the journey, De Villeneuve had to stay behind and was replaced by Kawahara Keiga (1786 - after 1859), a Japanese draughtsman, who was to make a vast number of drawings of plants, animals and all sorts of typical Japanese crafts. Fifty-seven Japanese men also accompanied them, and this group included several of Siebold's students who must have provided him with invaluable assistance in his research.

Siebold and Bürger were well prepared for the trip and had gathered together all sorts of equipment to take with them. This list included barometers, hygrometers, thermometers, chronometers, sextants, microscopes, furniture, crockery, silver, fine glassware, and even a piano. Some of these items were for their own use, while others were intended as gifts. They performed all manner of land surveying en route, and little escaped the attention of this inquisitive researcher. He wrote notes about everything, even people with unusual features, 'I was quite impressed by the unique structure of the face of an eighteen-year old boy. His nose was so small and his chin so prominent that if one drew a straight line between his chin and forehead, the tip of his nose would fall well behind it.' He treated many ill people on the way, too. Many of the poorer people had chronic skin- and eye diseases and syphilis. They were not allowed to deviate from the official route, which was difficult for Siebold because he was constantly excited by what he saw during the journey, and he would often leave the retinue with a number of attendants so that he could make his observations undisturbed. The guards had gradually become convinced of his purely scientific intentions and were sometimes willing to look the other way while he went about his unscheduled activities. One such unannounced excursion to visit an important magistrate led to this official being placed under house arrest for a year.

Siebold was amazed by to what degree some of the Japanese were obsessed with the Dutch language and culture – a few even went so far as to adopt a completely Dutch lifestyle. They paid a visit to the Mayor of Shimonoseki, Itō Jun, who had been given the name Van Den Berg by former *Opperhoofd* Doeff. Van Den Berg received his guests in a room that was furnished precisely according to European style. He proudly displayed his collection of curiosities, which included a variety of Dutch objects like furniture, weapons, clocks, crockery and even an unusual, pointed wig. He was dressed from head to toe in Dutch clothing, and his velvet coat with gold braiding, an embroidered waistcoat and short trousers, silk socks, hat and walking stick with a gold handle were apparently gifts from Doeff, who had worn them during his audience with the shogun.

27. The shogun. After an illustration in an old Japanese book. This is a fictive picture, as it was forbidden to make portraits of the shogun, taken from Nippon.

Siebold received a number of objects on his journey, which were probably of some interest to him. Someone brought him a miscarried deer foetus, as well as a live white deer. Both of these seemed to be albinos and he had to pay dearly to get them. One of his servants brought him a salamander that he had caught on the road. Siebold managed to ship two live specimens of this species *(Salamandra maxima)* to Holland, and it made him famous throughout Europe. He hardly had time to record all his observations in his diary; something he usually did while sitting in one of the uncomfortable sedan chairs, or 'small flying studies', as he liked to call them.

They arrived in Edo on 10 April, two months after their departure from Nagasaki. They had to wait a few days for their audience with the shogun so they passed the time visiting some interesting people who were keen to meet them. Among these were the Court Physician Katsuragawa Hoken, or Yoshichika (1797-1844), who had been given the Dutch name of Wilhelmus Botanicus, and a Japanese officer called Pieter van der Stolp. Both of these men had received their Dutch names from Doeff. They also mentioned a Japanese merchant Van Gulpen, who was a great admirer of Holland. Apparently, the former *Opperhoofd* Romberg had given him the name Adriaan Pauw, but he had tired of it and had asked Doeff for a new one.

The audience with the shogun was eventually held on 1 May 1826. Siebold wrote detailed descriptions in his diary of how he was taken, together with Lieutenant Colonel De Sturler and Dr. Bürger in a festive procession across bridges, through galleries and beautifully decorated entranceways to the audience hall.

28. Country folk and merchants, after a painting by Kawahara Keiga, taken from Nippon.

29. View of the harbour at Shimonoseki, after a painting by Kawahara Keiga, taken from Nippon.

LANDLIEDEN. ✳ LANDLEUTE.

*30. Salamander hunt, painted on silk by Kawahara
Keiga (National Museum of Ethnology, Leiden).*

31. Salamandra
maxima, *taken from
the* Fauna Japonica.
*Siebold managed to get
two living specimens of
this salamander to
Holland. One of them
survived for years in
the Artis Zoo in
Amsterdam.*

De Sturler was the only one permitted to go ahead, throw himself to the ground and, bowing deeply, proffer his respects to the shogun. He finally admitted that he did not actually manage to see the shogun, however. Immediately after this, the three of them had to pay their respects to a number of other dignitaries. Siebold observed:

> *None of these gentlemen were at home, so we had to sit on torturous seats, receive the compliments of their secretaries instead, and put up with being stared at. We were obliged to smoke tobacco, drink tea, eat confectionery, write epigrams and show off everything that we were wearing and carrying everywhere that we went. We eventually returned to our inn at nine o'clock that evening, having spent the entire day in our uncomfortable clothes, our legs aching from all the squatting and bowing, and with throbbing heads and upset stomachs.*[10]

32. Lacquered box with a picture of a moxa *treatment. (National Museum of Ethnology, Leiden).*

Siebold took advantage of the time the envoys spent discussing the copper trade to contact scholars, who showed him their work and took him to libraries. The Court Acupuncturist Ishizaka Sōtetsu (1779-1863) gave him a treatise on acupuncture and *moxa*. Siebold later published it as *Some information about acupuncture (The art of healing by needles); Drawn from a letter from the imperial acupuncturist of Japan, Isi Saka Sotels* [Ishizaka Sōtetsu] in the

Transactions of the Batavian Society of Arts and Sciences.[11] It contained a note from Sōtetsu in which he expressed his gratitude that he could, in his turn, enrich Western medicine with this contribution to it. The geographer Mogami Tokunai (1755-1836), who frequently visited North Japan from the end of 1785 at the request of the shōgunate, supplied Siebold with copious amounts of information regarding the Ainu language as well as details of his research trips to Sachalin in 1785 and 1786. According to Siebold, these two trips were extremely important, as they provided the Japanese with their first geographical knowledge of Krafto, which is what they called Sachalin. This was also how he discovered that Sachalin was an island, and not connected to the Asian mainland as many in Europe thought. He gleaned additional information from another geographer, Mamiya Rinzō (1780-1844), who had

33. Mogami Tokunai, who supplied Siebold with important geographical maps, including one of the island of Sachalin, taken from Nippon.

MOGAMI TOKUNAI.

最上德内

34. Map of the island of Sachalin at the mouth of the Amur River, probably dating from 1808 and made by Mamiya Rinzō. It was Rinzō who told Siebold that Sachalin was not connected to the mainland, as was believed in Europe at the time. (Library, Leiden University).

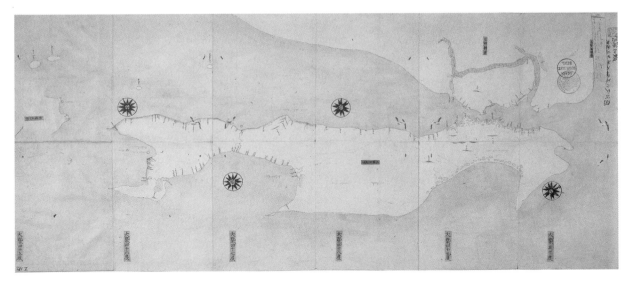

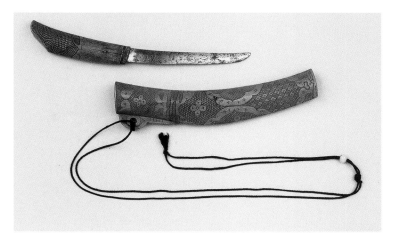

35. A tobacco box, tonkotsu, *made from wood, with Ainu motifs. (National Museum of Ethnology, Leiden).*

36. Ainu knife and scabbard. (National Museum of Ethnology, Leiden).

travelled frequently to Hokkaido and the northern regions of Japan, and had even made contact with the Russians. Siebold considered that these two men had made highly significant contributions to the fields of geography and ethnology, as is apparent from this quote from his book *Nippon:* 'It is thanks to these two men, whose passion for science, thirst for knowledge, courage and perseverance increased our knowledge of the islands of North Japan up to the mouth of the Amur River, not only in their own country but in Europe as well.' Siebold was given maps of the region and the surrounding sea, and he had copies made of them later.

It was perhaps his friendship with Takahashi Sakuzaemon, or Takahashi Kageyasu (1785-1829) that was his most important. Sakuzaemon, who had been given the name Globius by Doeff, was the Court Astronomer and Supervisor of the Imperial Library. He had been busy producing maps of the country for years, and had come into contact with the Dutch because one of his duties was to translate Dutch texts. Sakuzaemon was very impressed with Siebold's knowledge of astronomy, geography, botany and physics and the two men quickly forged a trusting relationship. Sakuzaemon was keen to find out anything he could about Europe and America, and he was enraptured by Siebold's accounts of the struggle of the North American Indians and Napoleon's exploits. He discovered that Siebold had a historical book about Napoleon, a travel journal by the Russian Krusenstern and maps of St. Petersburg, Holland and the Dutch colonies in his travel bag, and he was determined to have them translated into Japanese. At first, Siebold resisted but relented after Sakuzaemon proposed a trade of a topographic map of Japan and other maps of Japan and Ezo.
Supplying maps like these to foreigners was punishable by death, and Sakuzaemon was undoubtedly aware of this when he made the suggestion. He was motivated by the idea that translations of Siebold's books about Russia

37. The island of Jezo and the Japanese Kurile Islands, after an original map by Takahashi Sakuzaemon, drawn by Siebold. (Constantin von Brandenstein-Zeppelin, Schlüchtern, Germany).

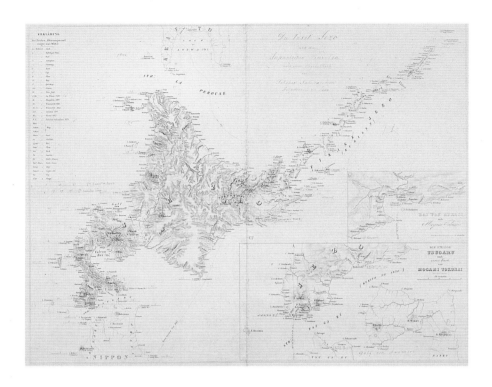

38. Painting by Katsushika Hokusai (1760-1849). Sudden shower, *1826. From a series depicting Japanese customs and festivities. It was ordered by Cock Blomhoff and either collected from Hokusai by Siebold, or someone delivered it to the Nagasakiya, where Siebold stayed. It is unclear whether Siebold actually met Hokusai. (National Museum of Ethnology, Leiden).*

would help defend his own country from a possible threat. This exchange occurred at a time when Russia was threatening Japan's northern borders, and he probably felt it was necessary to protect Japan from this menace.

On the other hand he considered the need to keep the maps a secret quite absurd, all the more because they were far less important than the contents of Siebold's books, and he ordered some officials to make copies of the maps, which he gave to Siebold. It is easy to understand how enticing this exchange must have been to Siebold. After all, Sakuzaemon was the best cartographer in Japan and his maps were perfect down to the minutest detail. Knowledge of Asia, Japan and its precise location in the area was still extremely limited. There was still no exact representation of the coastline of Northern Asia, despite the research conducted by the Russians, Krusenstern and Rezanov. Sakuzaemon and Siebold were so impassioned by their craving for knowledge, that they were prepared to stake their lives for it. Ultimately, the maps that passed hands in this exchange were to bring about their eventual downfall.

The relationship between Siebold and the Court Physician Habu Genseki (1762-1848) was to have similarly dramatic consequences. Genseki was fully aware of Siebold's highly successful cataract operations and was determined, at any cost, to obtain the formulation of the medicine that induced pupil enlargement, which would mean he could perform better eye surgery himself. Again, Siebold resisted for a while, but eventually agreed to supply the information – this time for an extremely dangerous object: a linen cloak decorated with the Imperial coat-of-arms. Genseki was also fully aware of the possible consequences of his actions but considered healing the sick to be paramount to abiding by the law.

Siebold's encounters and discussions provided him with so much information that he wanted to extend his stay in Edo. A number of scholars and interpreters made an official request for an extension to the authorities, but they did not receive a favourable reply. The rules were strict and travellers were required to stick to their itinerary. Besides this, there were a number of important people in Kyoto and Osaka that they had to visit on the return journey. The delegation finally left Edo on 18 May 1826 after a lavish farewell party and headed back to Nagasaki. Once again, they made intensive use of their sextants and chronometers. The Japanese officials were quite obliging and allowed them to undertake all sorts of research. They were fully aware of the fact that Siebold had hidden a compass inside his hat, and if they thought he was going to do something forbidden, did it on his behalf. His Japanese travelling companions co-operated with him because they were also excited by the interesting results yielded by the research, and they gradually altered their political ideas and saw through the futility of the regulations imposed by the Japanese authorities. Siebold could not have conducted any meaningful research without their collaboration. It transpired that measuring the height of Mount

Fuji was a major transgression for which they would later be held accountable. Fortunately, Siebold occasionally managed to put his research to one side and indulge in more earthly pursuits. His diary contains an entry, which mentions a visit he received from two stunningly beautiful women; and another where he writes of a night spent at a friend's house, again in the company of two well-brought up and entertaining ladies.

The trip back progressed somewhat more smoothly than the outward journey; De Sturler urged the delegation to proceed as quickly as possible, and they arrived on Deshima on 7 July 1826. The relationship between Siebold and De Sturler had not improved during the court journey. At first, De Sturler had heaped praise on the young scientist, but he became increasingly more unpleasant as his jealousy intensified when he saw the enthusiasm which greeted Siebold everywhere they went. He was also disappointed by the fact that, despite his successes in curing others of their ailments, Siebold had been unable to treat the infirmities he suffered from himself. It had become clear that De Sturler would soon leave Japan, not least because of the hard line he took towards the private business transactions conducted between Japanese and Dutch officials. This resulted in the Governor of Nagasaki banishing him and he was obliged to return to Batavia. However, even the distance between them did not prevent him from harassing Siebold and he even tried have him fired from the service because he was of the opinion that the results of his work were rather disappointing. The plants and seeds Siebold sent to Batavia were never good enough or were of known species. A friend advised Siebold to remain calm and to forge an amicable relationship with the new *Opperhoofd* on Deshima, Germain Felix Meijlan (1785-1831). Meijlan stopped private trade and instead established the 'Private Trade Association' *(Particuliere Handelssociëteit)*, which fell under his authority and ensured that the officials at the trading post and the crew of Dutch ships had an equal share of the business.

39. View of the Eitaibashi across the Sumida River in Edo (Tokyo). After a painting by Kawahara Keiga, taken from Nippon.

40.
Programme of
the Kabuki play
Onna teikun
Imoseyama
that Siebold
saw being
performed in
Osaka on his
return from
Edo during the
court journey.

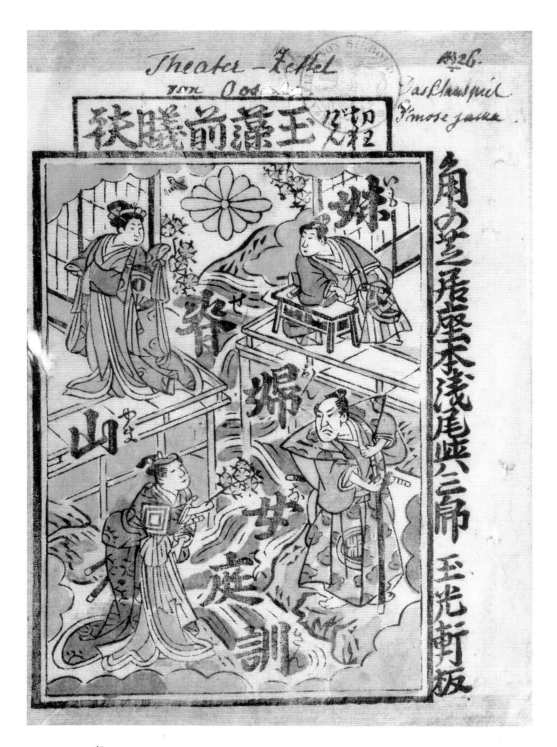

The Siebold incident

Siebold's botanical, zoological and ethnographic collection grew by leaps and bounds because of the court journey. The authorities in the Dutch East Indies decided on 20 June 1827 that Siebold should return to Batavia or The Netherlands, where he was to dedicate himself to cataloguing and describing his various collections, some of which had already been shipped to Holland. The rest of his objects would follow during the course of 1828. 'I have never felt as satisfied and cheerful as I do now,' wrote Siebold to his mother on Boxing Day, 1827. Meijlan was also extremely satisfied and reported to the Governor-General of Batavia, 'I have taken another look at his extensive collection and, however limited my own knowledge of such matters may be, do not hesitate to report that it will be a veritable treasure for the Royal Museum [...].'

The ship from Batavia that was to transport Siebold and the second part of his collection arrived in Nagasaki during August of 1828. Dr. Bürger was to assume all of Siebold's official duties from 1 October. However, fate was to play a hand that would result in Siebold remaining in Japan for at least another year. On 18 September, a violent storm that developed into a devastating typhoon caused the vessel, the *Cornelis Houtman*, together with its cargo of 89 chests full of natural historical objects, to run aground. Siebold reported:

> *Our island Deshima and the countryside surrounding Nagasaki were ravaged, and thousands of boats and people came to grief. Entire villages were destroyed and a considerable number of people died as a consequence. Even the upper part of my house was severely damaged by the hurricane and I had just enough time to flee to the forecourt with a few other people, where we hid between some large wooden crates, waiting for the house to collapse. Large sections of the wall around Deshima and several houses and warehouses collapsed. Most of the roofs and public and private gardens, including my own botanical garden met with an unhappy end; all evidence of this terrible destruction. I crawled to De Villeneuve's house on my hands and knees, clinging to uprooted trees on the way, to see if I could borrow a lantern from him.*[12]

They managed to refloat the ship in December, and fortunately it transpired that the collection had only been slightly damaged. In the meantime, the Japanese authorities had been alerted to the fact that the ship was carrying illicit goods. Siebold was detained on suspicion of espionage and was subject to a lengthy investigation, as were all the Japanese with whom he had been in contact. The maps and geographical information he had obtained from the Court Astronomer, Takahashi Sakuzaemon constituted the major transgression. 'This matter was considered to be a most severe offence from the perspective of such a small-minded government,' remarked Siebold in a letter to his mother. It is not certain, but it can be considered a distinct possibility that one of the draughtsmen who had copied some of the maps for Takahashi Sakuzaemon – Siebold was convinced that it was Mamiya Rinzō – had had an altercation with him and informed the authorities, who subsequently searched the cargo, which had been cast ashore. This resulted in an exhaustive enquiry and most of the Japanese who had come into contact with Siebold during the court journey – there were about forty of them – were arrested, as were fifty interpreters and a number of his students. Sakuzaemon was thrown into jail, his teeth were smashed out so that he couldn't bite off his tongue, and he was prevented from injuring himself in any other way, thus rendering himself incapable of testifying. About fifteen other officials from Takahashi's circle were apprehended and many others were interrogated.

The Governor of Nagasaki interrogated Siebold at length, trying to find out the names of the people who had assisted him in his scientific research. He wrote to his mother, 'It is, and will remain impossible to make me reveal the names of my friends who assisted me with such modesty and discretion.' He even begged to be incarcerated in a Japanese jail for the rest of his life in return for the freedom of his Japanese friends, and as punishment for his transgressions.

A shogunal decree issued in Edo on 23 January 1829 restricted his freedom of movement to Deshima, and he was forbidden from leaving Japan. The support he was offered by his Japanese friends is aptly illustrated by the actions of Yoshio Tsūjirō (1788-1833), who usually assisted him with the translation of Japanese books. Tsūjirō warned him that his house was soon going to be searched. 'I will soon be known as the worst Japanese person to ever serve the Emperor,' he lamented, before urging Siebold to save what he could. He informed Siebold that he had also been arrested because he was Siebold's co-worker, and a friend of Takahashi Sakuzaemon. He had been allowed to go free on condition that he remove all the maps and books that were still in Siebold's house so they could be used as evidence. The two men agreed that Tsūjirō would take the maps that they had already duplicated to the authorities that same day. Siebold was to make copies of the other maps that night and Tsūjirō would then hand over the originals. The most important of these were the maps of Ezo and the Kurile Islands. His diary contains the following observation, 'I locked myself in my study for the afternoon and worked through the night making a faithful copy of the map. It was a difficult and laborious task, something I have never managed to do in such a short space of time, and an excellent example of willpower and pure endurance.' The next morning Siebold asked *Opperhoofd* Meijlan to conceal this copy for him in the archives at the trading post.

Luckily it took longer than they had anticipated for the raid to occur, so Siebold had time to copy more maps, which he put in metal containers and was able to hide along with some texts and books. He hid one of these boxes in a hole in the wall of one of his rooms. They discovered later that rats had devoured the contents. He hid other maps in the animal pens adjacent to his house, and he even carried some about with him, concealed under his clothing. He hid weapons and daggers in the sliding doors and inside the double base of his flower box. In this way, he was able to save a considerable portion of his collection before the house was searched ten days later.

The investigation into his activities lasted longer than a year. Siebold refused to name a single 'accomplice', which earned him a great deal of respect. The frequency of the interrogations gradually decreased and many of the detainees were released in June 1829. Siebold was also granted more freedom of movement and his investigation continued, although at a much slower tempo. A verdict was eventually reached on 22 October 1829: no evidence had been produced which could justify the charges of espionage, and his services to Japan had to be taken into consideration. There was no denying that he had severely broken the rules, even if it had happened because of his scientific zeal. A decree was issued which banned him from Japan for life, and fifty of the Japanese who had been convicted of collusion were found guilty and sentenced. Some were imprisoned or were banished to remote islands, while others were forbidden from entering Edo. Takahashi Sakuzaemon died in prison of an unspecified illness before the sentence of death was passed on him on 20 March 1829. His son was banished to an island because of his father's misdemeanour. Habu Genseki, the Imperial Physician who had given Siebold the cloak with the Imperial coat-of-arms in exchange for the miracle cure that was used during eye operations, was removed from his post. His son was also punished. One of Takahashi Sakuzaemon's subordinates, who had committed suicide during the course of the investigation, had his salary posthumously withheld. Others, who perhaps should have felt responsible for his suicide, were sentenced to thirty days in prison because of his deed. The list of punishments appeared to be almost endless.

Siebold considered his banishment an extremely severe punishment, and although he had already made plans to return to Holland and start cataloguing and documenting his collection, it meant that he could never return to Japan, nor would he ever be able to see his beloved wife and child again. Sonogi had remained faithful to him throughout his ordeal; she had boundless admiration for him and supported him to the end. Siebold suffered terribly because of the unbearable knowledge that he would never see Sonogi or their two-year old daughter again. Before he left he had a lacquered box made with portraits of Sonogi and Oine on it, and he took locks of their hair, which he treasured.

41. Lacquered box with a picture of Sonogi (National Museum of Ethnology, Leiden).

42. Lacquered box with a picture of Oine (National Museum of Ethnology, Leiden).

Oine was two years and eight months old when Siebold left Japan on 30 December 1829. He asked two of his students, Kō Ryōsai (1799-1846) and Ninomiya Keisaku (1804-1862), to share the responsibilities of raising and educating his daughter. As the *Cornelis Houtman* left the harbour the following morning, a small fishing boat appeared from out of the mist. When at last he could discern who the passengers were, he saw that it was his wife with their child and the two students, who had come to bid him a final farewell. His sadness at leaving his beloved family and Japan knew no bounds. He carried the little lacquered box with their pictures on it everywhere he went, and would later include a portrait that De Villeneuve had made of his wife and daughter in his book *Nippon*.

43. Letter from Siebold to Sonogi, dated Leiden, 25 December 1830. (Constantin von Brandenstein-Zeppelin, Schlüchtern, Germany).

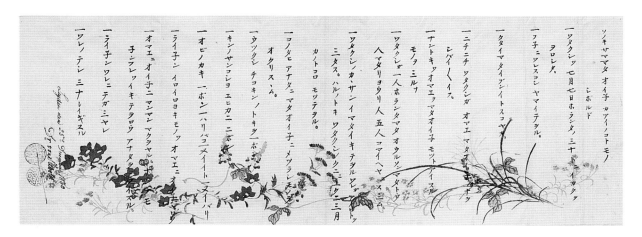

The Leiden period

Siebold arrived in Batavia on 28 January 1830 and received permission to leave on the first ship to Holland. It set sail on 5 March and he stepped ashore in The Netherlands sometime around the middle of July. He was deeply touched when he heard that King Ludwig of Bavaria, who ruled from 1825-1848 had pleaded for his release with the shogun of Japan. His reception in Holland was also very warm and enthusiastic, and King Willem I allowed him all the time and space he needed to organise and catalogue his collection. He received *carte blanche* to deal with it as he thought fit, despite the fact that he had accumulated it while in the service of the Dutch government. This turned out to be a good idea, because it's accommodation had not yet been arranged, not least because the Blomhoff Collection had filled the Royal Cabinet of Curiosities to bursting. At the same time, the government informed him that a Royal decree had been issued, which guaranteed they would buy the ethnographic collection for about 60.000 guilders, of which he was to receive a 12.000 guilder advance immediately. His ethnographic collection consisted of approximately 5000 objects. His natural history collection included 200 mammals, 900 birds, 750 fish, 170 reptiles and more than 5000 invertebrates. He had also accumulated 2000 different types of plants and 12.000 dried plant specimens.

Siebold was nominated for a knighthood in the Order of the Dutch Lion *(Orde van den Nederlandschen Leeuw)* on 11 April 1831. The Dutch East Indies Army appointed him to the post of Superintendent Officer of Health on 20 April. The first thing Siebold wanted to do was write his book, *Nippon*, so the copious and time-consuming task of documenting his collections was designated to his assistant, A. Hakbijl. Before Hakbijl could start doing this however, Siebold had to retrieve those objects from his collections that he had stored in Antwerp. He had also sent a number of crates containing dried plants, seeds and different types of wood to the National Herbarium in Brussels before his departure from Japan. He considered it a good idea to have these objects returned to Holland as the provinces of Wallonia and Flanders had recently declared themselves an independent country called Belgium. The prevailing unrest prevented him from returning to Holland with a collection of about 250 live plants that he had left in the botanical gardens in Ghent, which was an important centre for the study of ornamental plants. Sixty-five of these plants were eventually returned to him in 1841. The greater parts of his collections were already in Holland, mostly undamaged, and were kept at the Museum of

44. *King Willem I.*

45. Gecco jamori, *taken from the* Fauna Japonica *(above right).*

46. Nycthereutus viverrinus, *the* tanuki *or racoon, taken from the* Fauna Japonica.

47. Halcyon coromanda major, *taken from the* Fauna Japonica.

48. Ibis nippon, *taken from
the* Fauna Japonica.

Natural History in Leiden. Many live plants were being taken care of in the botanical gardens supervised by Professor Karl Ludwig Blume (1796-1862) at Leiden University. Blume had been the director of *'s Lands Plantentuin*, the botanical garden in Buitenzorg on Java from 1822 to 1826, and had worked with Siebold for years.

These developments made Siebold decide to go and live in Leiden, and it appears that he was offered the opportunity of teaching at Leiden University; something he declined. As he wrote to his mother:

> *You are mistaken if you think I have any interest in becoming a lecturer. It is something that would reflect badly on my career. Why on earth would I dedicate myself to such extraneous activities without needing to, when I can easily spend ten years publishing my works on Japan? Why would I enslave myself to time and trap myself in a lecture-hall preaching like a schoolmaster to deaf ears, when I can live as a free man and do as I please?* [13]

The Rapenburg

Siebold rented a house at 19 Rapenburg in 1832. He stored a significant part of his ethnographic collection here and made it accessible to the public, calling it his 'Japanese Museum'. This house, much like the one in Narutaki, became a focal point for all sorts of scholars. He had maintained contact with Bürger, who still lived on Deshima, and with his successors, who sent new plants and cuttings to Holland whenever Siebold requested them. He made similar requests to *'s Lands Plantentuin*, which cultivated many Japanese plant varieties. Some frowned at the quantities he requested, and questioned whether they were intended more for commercial use than for scientific research.

The first chapters of his opus, *Nippon* and sections of his *Fauna Japonica* and *Bibliotheca Japonica* were to appear over the next few years. Kuo Ch'êng-chang, a Chinese who had travelled with him from Batavia, and who was to eventually work with him for seven years, helped him with his cataloguing and linguistic studies. Soon after he returned to Europe, Siebold had made the acquaintance of the German philologist Johann Joseph Hoffmann (1805-1878) in Antwerp, who also hailed from Würzburg and travelled about as a theatrical singer. He would also become one of Siebold's loyal colleagues. Hoffman took Chinese and Japanese lessons from Kuo Ch'êng-chang, and after a few months started translating Japanese texts.

Siebold made a number of trips to a variety of European capitals in 1834 and 1835. He did this primarily for financial reasons, as the initial instalment of 12.000 guilders he had received from the Dutch government for his collection was not enough to pay for the publication of his texts. He might also have

49. The house Siebold bought at Rapenburg 19.

50. The Chinese, Kuo Ch'êng-chang, taken from Nippon.

made the trips in order to promote the first volume of *Nippon*, which he had recently finished. He met numerous scholars who imparted relevant information to him that he could incorporate in his publications, including the famous Russian, Admiral von Krusenstern (1770-1846) in St. Petersburg. Krusenstern had circumnavigated the coasts of Japan during his voyages around the world and had made maps of the region. Siebold also managed to pre-sell ten copies of his book *Nippon* to Tsar Nicholas I. While in Berlin he met several well-known scholars, like the zoologist Christian Gottfried Ehrenberg (1795-1876) and the explorer and natural researcher Alexander von Humboldt (1769-1859). He also met the old Emperor, Franz I (1768-1835), and his wife, in Vienna and continued in this way to add to his ever-increasing circle of friends and acquaintances. The trip was a success and attracted more attention to him and his scientific work, which yielded vital support.

Siebold had meanwhile invested significant funds expanding his ethnographic collection. He approached the Dutch King in 1837, requesting that the pledge to buy his collection be fulfilled. Jan Cock Blomhoff (1779-1843), a former *Opperhoofd* on Deshima, and Johan Frederik van Overmeer-Fisscher (1800-1848), who had been a Warehouse Master on Deshima had also amassed their own collections of Japanese objects. These were kept at the Royal Cabinet of Curiosities *(Koninklijk Kabinet van Zeldzaamheden)* in The Hague, and Siebold proposed in his letter to the King that they be combined with his own collection so that a large Museum of Ethnology could be established. A Royal decree issued on 18 June 1838 ordered that the remaining sum of 42.000 guilders – he had received an amount of 6000 guilders in the meantime – be paid to him in four instalments over as many years. The proposed museum had to wait until an appropriate building became available.

In 1836, Siebold had the opportunity of buying the house on the Rapenburg, which he had been renting, for 13.000 guilders. He had already sub-let the ground floor to a students' association, called 'Minerva,' that same year, which meant that he had moved to the first floor. Some of the rooms on this floor had also been rented, to no less than six people; Siebold did not stay in the house much himself. The subsequent shortage of space meant that part of his ethnographic collection had to be relocated to a storage space on the Paardensteeg, a street that no longer exists. The comments in his guest book, which is now stored in the Leiden University Library, are a testimony to the number of dignitaries who came to view his collection. There is effusive praise from the Russian *tzarevitch*, Alexander, who later became Tsar Alexander II (1818-1881), King Willem II (1792-1849) and Friedrich Wilhelm IV from Prussia. His colleagues were also highly impressed by his collection. The physician Ewald Hasse wrote in his memoirs:

> *I went to Leiden many times. Franz von Siebold, 'the Japanese' who I met in Vienna, had established himself there. His spacious house was filled with a wealth of objects he had brought with him from Japan. All of his crockery, some of his furniture, the paintings on the walls and other household items all came from Japan. He cultivated plants from this island empire, and a lively, scruffy monkey, indigenous to Japan, was chained to a tree in the garden. The small, ugly Chinaman who was there would be a good match for the monkey [sic], but in fact he was introduced to me as an educated gentleman, whom Siebold had persuaded with great effort to assist him with the publication of his opus Nippon.*[14]

Nippon

In 1840 Siebold purchased a plot of land near to the Zijlpoort in Leiden, where he had a house and a hothouse built for him. He called it 'Nippon' and planted a small botanical garden where he cultivated some of the plants and seeds he had brought with him from Japan. Many Asiatic plants, such as peony roses, chrysanthemums and lilies, as well as a variety of shrubs and trees that can now be found throughout Europe, had their origins in this garden. He also supplied the botanical gardens at Leiden University with countless plants, shrubs and trees. Some of these, which were actually planted by Siebold, like the gigantic ginkgo-tree, can still be seen today.

Siebold usually spent the winter in Germany, as the Dutch climate had a bad effect on his health. He met Helene Ida Caroline, Baroness von Gagern (1820-1877), who was twenty-five years his junior, while staying at a health resort in Bad Kissingen during the winter of 1840. Siebold was fifty years old when they married five years later, in July 1845. He took his wife with him to his house in Leiderdorp, and built his mother a small house, called *Achterland bij Nippon* ('Hinterland at Nippon'), on his estate. His mother died in 1845, shortly after she moved there.

His wife's health also started to deteriorate because of the damp climate, so they decided that they would only stay at 'Nippon' during the summer and bought the former Franciscan Monastery of St. Martin near Boppard am Rhein. They had five children: Alexander (1846-1911), Helene (1848-1927), Mathilde (1850-1906), Heinrich (1852-1908) and Maximiliaan (1854-1887). Their sons Alexander and Heinrich would inherit their father's interest in Japan.

51. 'Nippon', the villa Siebold had built on a piece of ground he bought in 1840 on the Lage Rijndijk in the former village of Leiderdorp. The house was demolished in 1893 due to the expansion of the city of Leiden. Siebold Street and Decima Street are currently situated on the former nursery grounds.
(Municipal Archives, Leiden)

53. Helene von Siebold-
von Gagern, at the age of
24 years, painted by Oscar
Begas. (Constantin von
Brandenstein-Zeppelin,
Schlüchtern, Germany)

52. Helene von Siebold-
von Gagern (1820-1877).
(Municipal Archives,
Leiden)

54. Portrait of Siebold when he was a colonel in the general staff of
the Dutch East Indies Army, after an original by H.R. Heidemans
in 1848. (Municipal Archives, Leiden)

54a. Title-page Nippon.

55. Catching fish, after a painting by Kawahara Keiga, taken from Nippon.

Nippon

Siebold presented the Society of Dutch Letters (*Maatschappij der Nederlandsche Letterkunde*) with the first copy of what was to become known as his *magnum opus, Nippon*, on 26 November 1833. He started working on the book soon after his collection and his complete reference library arrived in Leiden. His purpose was clear, as is also indicated by the sub-title: it was to be a collection of individual essays on a variety of different topics. Siebold considered that this was the only way he could do justice to the existing body of works, many of which came from Japan, as well as to the scientific inclination to occasionally over-elaborate. He considered that this intention justified the sub-title: *Archives for the description of Japan and its depending and tributary countries: Jezo with the Southern Kurile Islands, Krafto, Korea and the Loochoo Islands, compiled from Japanese and European writings, as well as my own personal observations.*[15] He also assumed the role of publisher and, according to the imprint, the book was printed in 1832 by J. Muller & Company in Amsterdam and C.C. van der Hoek in Leiden. This date is highly improbable, because further research has shown that Siebold only presented the first copy in the autumn of 1833. The date becomes even more unlikely because of the note on the title page, which states that he was a Knight of the Royal Order of Citizens of Merit of Crown of Bavaria *(Ridder in de Koninklijke Orde van Verdienstelijke Burgers van de Beierse Kroon)*. Siebold was only awarded this distinction on 30 November 1832. In addition, his former patron, Nees von Esenbeck, who had admitted him to the Imperial Leopoldinic Carolinic Academy of Natural History *(Kaiserlich Leopoldinisch-Carolinischen Akademie der Naturforscher)* in Vienna in 1822, wrote Siebold a letter on 15 January 1834 thanking him for the first two volumes, which he had just received. It seems, therefore, that the first two volumes came out in the autumn of 1833, the third most likely in January 1835, and the fourth in February 1835. The volumes after this appeared very sporadically and sometimes with large intervals between them. The last volume appears to have been printed despite not being finished, because Siebold was too busy preparing for his second trip to Japan in 1859. (The German edition of *Nippon* is actually the only complete version; only one volume appeared in Dutch. Some parts were translated into French and Russian; a complete Japanese translation was made later.) His sons prepared a corrected and expanded edition in 1897, which incorporated much of the material in the manuscripts that Siebold had not used, and Dr. Trautz edited a still more expanded third edition in 1930-1931. The first volume of *Nippon* is primarily concerned with Japan's geography, and contains the results of the countless measurements he made together with his assistant Bürger. It also included his observations about different types of rock, soil composition, the sulphur content of warm springs and the various altimetrical statistics that many of his students had recorded. The Dutch edition only contained a scant selection of these data, together with extracts from the third volume.

56. Masked dancers, after a painting by Kawahara Keiga, taken from Nippon.

*57. The doctors'
house on Deshima.
Illustration from*
Souvenir du Japon,
Van Lijnden, 1860.

*58. View of the
entertainment
district in Nagasaki.
Painting by
Kawahara Keiga
(made between
1823 -1825).
(National Museum
of Ethnology,
Leiden).*

The second volume contained a comprehensive account of the court journey that Siebold made in 1826. Indeed it was so detailed that a short overview of the trip took 30 pages and general observations on local customs, ships, bridges and so on were covered in 19 pages. The rest of the book – a total of 146 pages – was dedicated to only describing the land journey across Kyushu and the voyage over the Inland Sea of Japan to the harbour at Muro.

The reader has to resort to the brief notes written by Siebold's sons for the rest of this account, which appeared in a later edition of the book. Siebold seems to have been obsessed with all sorts of geodesy, and complained that the journey could not be extended, thus providing him with enough time to gather more accurate data. He proposed that the return journey from Edo to Kyoto follow the considerably longer Kisokaidō route, so that he would have an opportunity to see more of the country's interior. He was not particularly impressed by the excursions to places of interest, proposed with all good intentions by their Japanese escorts. He mentions absolutely nothing of the *Opperhoofd's* conduct, and his humour only seems to have improved when he met sick people or local doctors, who had come to ask the 'Miracle Doctor' for advice. Readers who endure these sections will be rewarded with all sorts of interesting observations. Most of the illustrations are based on the work of Kawahara Keiga, who Siebold also called Tojoske (Toyosuke), describing him as, 'a very gifted artist from Nagasaki, highly proficient in drawing plants, who also started to use European techniques in his portraits and landscapes.' Later volumes, especially those concerned with the Buddhist pantheon, the literature, and the history of Japan were mostly based on the translations Hoffman made for him from a variety of Japanese texts. Sometimes these were nothing more than short texts together with illustrations by lithographers like J.J.Cernet, Francois Desterbecq (1807-1849?), J. Erxleben (active from1832-1838), Henri Philippe Heidemans (1803?-1864?), A.E. Saagmans Mulder (1804-1841), Ludwig Nader (1811?-1840) and P.C. Tesch (active from 1832-1849), who made adaptations of original drawings and paintings by Kawahara Keiga and De Villeneuve. It seems that after he had finished the first two volumes, Siebold was hardly able to complete this monumental work, which was supposed to consist of nine large volumes. A selection from the volumes available at the time was translated into French by A. de Montry en E. Fraissinet. It was published in five volumes between the years 1838 and 1840 and included a botanical atlas. A Russian translation of selections from the first two volumes appeared in 1840.

Advisor to the King

In 1842, King Willem II bestowed the rank of noble upon Siebold because of his public services, and he was allowed to call himself 'Esquire'. He was also appointed to the position of 'Advisor to the King on Japanese Affairs', a task he performed with great seriousness. From that moment on he bombarded the Dutch government with proposals aimed at improving their relations with Japan. Siebold predicted that the search for new markets by rapidly developing countries like the United States and Great Britain would mean that Japan ran the danger of being forced to trade with the rest of the world. The Opium Wars in China clearly illustrated this. Siebold wanted to open Japan up to the rest of the world on friendly terms before it was too late. He pointed out that many people in Japan were keen to adopt an open-door policy, most especially from a scientific point of view, and he thought it a good idea to approach them from this angle, allowing trade to follow as a natural consequence. Holland was probably the ideal country to initiate such a move because of the long-standing amicable relationship that existed between the two countries. Siebold composed a letter, dated 15 February 1844, which would be presented to the Japanese authorities on behalf of the King of Holland. This letter was taken to Nagasaki on the frigate *Palembang* in July 1844 and handed over to the Governor of Nagasaki by Pieter Albert Bik, who was *Opperhoofd* at the time. Siebold wrote the text for the letter, which Willem II used verbatim, and which, briefly summarised, stated the following: The King presented himself as representing all nations who wanted to trade with Japan. Now that international traffic between nations was rapidly increasing, a policy of isolationism might arouse enmity among some countries. He asked that the laws restricting trade and commerce be more flexible, and that the harbours be made accessible to foreigners to avoid the threat of war. Peace could only be guaranteed by maintaining friendly relations and free trade. In conclusion, he thanked the shogun for the hospitality that Holland had enjoyed for the last two centuries.

This letter made a great impression on shogun Ieyoshi, who sent a reply a year later, on 4 July 1845, in which he expressed his heartfelt thanks to the King for his concern. However, he was obliged to honour the holy laws of his forefathers and could not adopt an open-door policy. Holland would remain the only nation that could continue to trade with Japan. He also sent sixteen folding-screens with beautiful paintings on a gold background to Willem II as a reciprocal gift to thank him for the many presents he had sent. These are preserved in the National Museum of Ethnology *(Rijksmuseum voor Volkenkunde)* in Leiden. The letter from the shogun, which was also written on gold paper and placed in a lacquered box, is now preserved at the National Archives *(Algemeen Rijksarchief)* in The Hague. The shogun's refusal did not

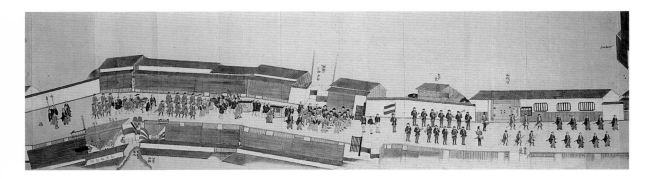

59. The official presentation of a letter from King Willem II to the Governor of Nagasaki in 1844. Detail from a scroll measuring 5,40 m long and 37,5 cm high. Two officers, walking behind the Junior Officer carrying the flag, hold the box with the letter, and a third carries the box containing the key. Opperhoofd *Pieter Albert Bik, Colonel Coops and several ships' officers and trading post officials follow them. (Collection Netherlands Maritime Museum, Amsterdam)*

prevent Siebold from urging the Dutch government to continue pressurising Japan into opening its borders, thus avoiding certain trouble. However, it was to little avail.

The opening of Japan

There was also growing concern in Japan regarding the situation of the country. Various *daimyō* were becoming aware of the increasing attempts by foreign ships to enter Japanese waters, and some of the shogun's advisors had started to stress the importance of reconsidering Japan's approach to the international situation.

In the meantime, reports from the United States revealed that they were planning an expedition to Japan. The expansion of their whaling industry into the north-western areas of the Pacific Ocean resulted in more and more of their ships being stranded on the Japanese coasts, and the crew members had to endure great hardships. The Japanese even opened fire on the ships that were sent to collect them. America decided that the time had come to exert even more pressure on Japan to open its borders. Their earlier attempts had been unsuccessful, so they decided that a show of force should be made by the forthcoming expedition. Siebold was fully aware of these developments and warned the Dutch government that they would have to act quickly if they were to retain their privileged relationship with Japan. He sent a draft treaty to the Minister of Colonies with the request that he forward it to Japan. This document contained a proposal that, for the time being, only Nagasaki be opened up to Dutch- and other foreign ships. Various influential people, including Prince Hendrik, the brother of King Willem II, praised the proposal, but a majority in the Cabinet decided to wait and see what happened. They opted instead to send the treaty to *Opperhoofd* Donker Curtius (1813-1879) with the instruction that he present it to a lower ranking official, namely the Governor of Nagasaki.

Siebold was so frustrated by this that he decided to offer his services outside of The Netherlands. When he heard about Russian plans to make contact with

Japan, he sent a copy of his latest volume of *Nippon*, which detailed the geography of the Northern Territories of Japan, including the Kurile Islands, Sachalin and East Siberia, to the Russian government and was promptly invited to St. Petersburg for talks by the Russian chancellor, Count Von Neselrode (1780-1862). Siebold, still an officer in the Dutch colonial army, felt that he was entitled to hold discussions of this nature with foreign governments despite their own imperialistic aspirations, as he was on exceptional leave at the time. Obviously, the Dutch government did not appreciate this attitude. He delivered what was by now a familiar message in St. Petersburg: try to negotiate a peaceful trade agreement with Japan, and send a delegation there to ensure that it is ratified. Von Neselrode, for his part, was to write a letter to the authorities in Edo in which he would urge them to open the Japanese ports to Russian ships.

Shortly after Siebold returned from Russia, a convoy of four warships arrived off the coast of Uraga. On 8 July 1853, Captain Matthew Galbraith Perry (1794-1858) delivered a letter from the American president, Filmore, addressed to the shogun, which contained the urgent message requesting that the country open its doors to international trade. Perry added a note of his own, stating that he would return in 1854 to collect the positive response. Von Neselrode's letter was presented to the Japanese on 21 September 1853.

Perry returned in February 1854 with a fleet of eight warships and Japan capitulated soon afterwards. The Treaty of Kanagawa was signed on 31 March 1854. It stated that the harbours of Shimoda and Hakodate would be accessible for limited commercial activity and that the Americans could establish a consulate in Shimoda.

Jan Hendrik Donker Curtius (1813-1879), who was *Opperhoofd* on Deshima at this time was furious at the disastrous consequences this would have for Dutch trade and he sent a letter to Holland, pointing an accusing finger at Siebold, whose works on Japan probably hastened these events.

Permanent Advisor on Japanese Affairs

In the meantime, Siebold had sold the Monastery of St. Martin near Boppard, in September 1853, and gone to live in Bonn. He continued working steadily on his books, inspired by the academic climate there, and lectured frequently at the university in the city. He was granted access to a garden where he cultivated a number of Japanese and Chinese plants, including several varieties of tea, edible thistles and mulberries.

When he heard that the Dutch government was interested in continuing to work out their trading arrangements with Japan, he again offered his services as an advisor to the Minister of Colonies. The Minister wrote to the King stating, 'One would have to agree that there is no one in Europe who has made such a thorough study of Japanese laws, conduct and customs as Siebold. The advice of a man like this in the areas of politics and trade would be considered extremely beneficial. In my opinion, his knowledge is also highly valued by foreign governments, which is something he could easily use to his own advantage.'

To be guaranteed of Siebold's services, the King would be obliged to appoint him to the governmental position of Permanent Advisor on Japanese Affairs. Siebold would have to dedicate himself to various political, commercial and scholarly problems that might arise. He could continue living in Bonn and would be compensated for his travelling and living expenses by the Dutch government. Needless to say, the King heeded this advice.

Siebold assumed his new responsibilities enthusiastically and immediately started producing all kinds of reports and advice, among them was one regarding the renewal of the permits that had been issued by the first shogun in 1609 and 1611. Another was concerned with the *Cambang*, the private business conducted by trading post officials and sailors that had always consisted of (privately) imported articles that were not part of the official VOC trade. Siebold wanted to include these in the official trading activities, and in 1855 requested that he be appointed as the director of the *Cambang*. He wanted to use this position to import products of a scientific nature in addition to the more commercial items, as well as continue to provide Japan with scientific and technological information. He considered that this was the only way Holland would be able to maintain its position of privilege in the European trade. This request was denied and the job was given to someone else who, in Siebold's opinion, was paid far too much. The profits realised from the *Cambang* were also excessive – sometimes as much as four hundred percent – and he thought this could only have a deleterious effect on the good reputation of the Dutch.

Some people found Siebold's inflated ego and meddlesome behaviour quite irritating and his proposals for advisory positions were gradually rejected more and more, with the message that someone else was already performing these functions. The government tried to compensate him by raising his annual wage from 4000 to 5000 guilders. Siebold's pride was injured by this proposal, which he considered extremely humiliating, and replied that he could only accept the offer if it was accompanied by a formal position at the Ministry of Colonies.

He refused a second offer of a wage increase in 1858. In the past, the Minister of Colonies had always kept Siebold well informed about Japan and the Dutch East Indies, as befitting his position as Advisor on Japanese Affairs. The new Minister did not do this and it annoyed Siebold so much that he refused to accept any salary at all, because it was impossible for him to do his work properly under such conditions. In addition, he felt he had made so many sacrifices while employed by the Dutch government that a bonus would be a more appropriate form of compensation, rather than a favour or any other financial assistance. He preferred to be fired from his present position if he was not given an official post. The Minister advised the King to refuse Siebold's request and to fire him, as the Ministry of External Affairs was due to assume the responsibility for Japanese affairs anyway. Siebold was dismissed in February 1858.

Even Siebold, stubborn as he was, realised he had finally gone too far and eventually sent a letter to the King, apologising for his obstinate behaviour. He explained that he had been hugely disappointed by the fact that he had never been offered a better position, despite promises that had been made to him in the past by the Ministry of Colonies. He was still prepared to devote himself to assisting in the intellectual development of the Japanese people, as well as to the exportation of Japanese commodities, so he asked to be taken back into the service. Although his services were not deemed so valuable any more – a trade agreement had been signed in 1855 and the Japanese harbours had been opened up – many thought that his earlier refusal had been influenced by his passion, and did not want to offend him any further. The King assented, and Siebold was re-employed on 26 May 1858, on an annual wage of 5000 guilders. Siebold also received the news that the order banishing him from Japan had been revoked in December of that same year.

60. Portrait of Siebold, probably painted by his daughter, Mathilde von Brandenstein in 1877, when she was 7 years old.

He started planning his return to the country he had left nearly thirty years before almost immediately. Just how much he missed Japan was evident from a letter he had written to a friend a few years earlier:

> *... I have never felt so restless and my thoughts seem to be tossed about by the stormy waters of the Pacific Ocean. In my mind I drift back to the Japanese island kingdom, for the country where I spent my scholarly youth, and which is now threatened by a European culture with all its horror and misery. When I think of Japan, so far away from my motherland, then the same glow that inspired me as a youth in 1822 courses through these sixty-year-old veins. The first time that I went there, it was to discover those secret treasures unknown to European science. Now my visit is spurred by the desire to assist and save this kind, brave and happy nation that I dragged from obscurity into this tumultuous world.*[16]

60a. The house of the trading post physician, where Siebold stayed from 1823 until 1829. Detail of the scale model that Blomhoff had built for him by craftsmen in Nagasaki in 1817 (Blomhoff Collection, National Museum of Ethnology, Leiden).

Siebold's second trip to Japan

Siebold had already suggested to the Minister in 1858 that it would be expedient to establish a Japanese Trading Company to accelerate their trade with Japan. The Minister referred him to the Netherlands Trading Company, who had thought of a similar plan. Siebold offered to represent them in East Asia, and advised them to start concentrating on trading with China, Siberia, Korea, the Ryukyu Islands and Taiwan. It was also imperative to establish a regular boat service between Shanghai and Nagasaki, and he ended by emphasising that the Dutch cultural influence should not be neglected. After lengthy consideration, they decided to send him to Japan for two years.

At the same time, Siebold requested that the Dutch government appoint him to the post of General Consul of the Netherlands in Japan, but they declined on the grounds that the two functions could not be combined. They offered him the task of delivering the trade agreement of 1855, which had meanwhile been worked out, to Japan for ratification. He would be paid 5000 guilders and receive another 2000 guilders to cover his expenses. Siebold, now 63 years old, was honoured by the prospect of performing such a service and he began in all earnest to prepare for his second trip to Japan. Scores of crates containing clothes, scientific apparatus, pharmacological instruments,

61. Dr. Conradus Leemans (1809-1893), who was the director of the Archaeological Cabinet (the present-day National Museum of Antiquities) and the temporary acting director of 'The National Japanese Museum Von Siebold'.

glassware, clocks and an entire printing press were made ready. He dearly wanted to introduce Western printing techniques to Japan, with the idea of organising the publication of a Dutch-Japanese dictionary. He also intended to gather as much information as he could to complete the latest edition of his atlas.

He left his nursery in Leiderdorp and his villa 'Nippon' in the care of his gardener Jacob Mater. He handed over his ethnographic collection to Dr. Conradus Leemans (1809-1893), the director of the Archaeological Cabinet *(Archeologisch Kabinet)*, the present-day National Museum of Antiquities. Leemans had the collection that was stored in the damp premises on the Paardensteeg transferred to a rented house on the Breestraat. The museum would henceforth be called 'The National Japanese Museum Von Siebold' *(Rijks Japansch Museum Von Siebold)*.

Just before he was about to leave, the Minister expressed his misgivings about dispatching a former outcast to Edo to hand over an important trade agreement. However, they resolved the situation by telling Siebold that the delivery of the treaty in Edo had absolute priority and could not wait for his other preparations. Siebold was somewhat disappointed by this, but not so much that it got in the way of his own preparations to leave. He published an elaborate letter in Germany and The Netherlands, which was addressed to his friends and scientific colleagues in which he substantiated his new intentions. The Austrian Imperial Leopoldinic-Carolinic Academy of National History was planning to establish a National Museum of Natural Science, and they had high expectations of his activities in Japan. Shortly before he died, the renowned explorer Alexander von Humboldt wrote a farewell letter to Siebold expressing his great admiration for his scientific accomplishments and wished him every success with his new plans.

Siebold left Europe in April 1859, accompanied by his thirteen-year-old son, Alexander. They arrived on 14 August, and stepped ashore in Nagasaki thirty years after Siebold's previous departure. His arrival this time was incomparable to his previous one: there were no inspectors or search parties waiting suspiciously on the shore to greet the new arrivals. Deeply moved, Siebold stepped onto the quay where the *Opperhoofd*, Dr. Jan Hendrik Donker Curtius was waiting for him. Donker Curtius invited Siebold to stay at his house until they found a suitable place for him to live. The *Opperhoofd's* house was the same as it had been thirty years before, as was the doctor's. The botanical garden was still there, but showed few signs of life, and it was with some difficulty that Siebold managed to free the now-overgrown memorial plaque he had placed there to honour Kaempfer and Thunberg. The sight of the garden brought with it a flood of memories of his earlier hardships, and he was filled with sadness. Donker Curtius had spent the last seven years on Deshima, and his stories only made Siebold even sadder.

He spoke of the changes in Japan and the feeble progress of Dutch trade. He recounted the fate of all those Japanese who had been punished because of Siebold's actions. Some had been banished or imprisoned, others had committed suicide or had fallen ill and died. Kō Ryōsai had also passed away, but his other pupil, Ninomiya Keisaku, who he had also asked to take care of his daughter, was still alive although he had been half-paralysed by a stroke.

62. Philipp Franz von Siebold with his oldest son, Alexander. (Municipal Archives, Leiden)

He too, had been waiting on the quay with members of his family and some of Siebold's former students. Siebold was deeply touched and most grateful for the help these two men had given his daughter, Oine. Of course, he saw Sonogi and Oine. Oine was thirty-two years old and had a daughter of her own, called Taka, and she ran a gynaecology clinic in Nagasaki. Sonogi had remarried after Siebold's departure from Japan, and had given birth to her second daughter in 1831. After her second husband died, she re-married again, this time to the merchant Tawaraya Toijiro, and bore him a son. Toijiro had also passed away before Siebold's arrival in Nagasaki. Sonogi ran a small oil business in the same building that Ninomiya used as his consulting rooms and surgical clinic. When he saw Sonogi and their daughter again after all these years, Siebold reassured them that he had thought about them every hour of each day for the thirty years they had been separated. He was very shocked when he heard that Sonogi had remarried twice in that time. Whether Siebold's second marriage, and the fact that he had five children by it, affected Sonogi in the same way is not known. The old sweethearts found solace by frequently exchanging pleasant memories. Siebold resumed his earlier activities with his few remaining friends and was able to travel extensively now that all the old restrictions had been lifted. Alexander was very impressed by the way in which so many Japanese people welcomed and respected his father. This was especially true of Ninomiya Keisaku, Siebold's most loyal friend, who had been imprisoned because he had measured the height of Mount Fuji for Siebold with an altimeter.

Donker Curtius informed Siebold about the political situation in Japan in detail, but he had little to say about the Dutch government's procrastination in securing a trade agreement. The trade in the Chinese and Japanese regions was firmly in the grip of the Americans and the British, and as Siebold had always suspected, they treated the country and the people with disdain because of their basic lack of knowledge about them. Indeed, they were not in the slightest bit interested in the Japanese culture, being concerned only with their commercial activities. Needless to say, this attitude was greatly resented by the Japanese, and Siebold was painfully aware of the hostile attitude they had adopted in their dealings with foreigners.

He did not gain much satisfaction from his work as an advisor to the Trading Company either, and had become more interested in politics, finding it difficult to restrict himself to purely scientific pursuits. He also found it hard to perform his duties as a physician: people seemed to be content to stand and wait on his porch until he decided to let them in. The ease with which he could again immerse himself in his previous lifestyle, gave him the distinct feeling that he had only been away for a few months, instead of thirty years. The only setback he experienced was a fire that broke out in the small temple he was using as his temporary lodgings, which damaged his hands and burned part of his face. He decided to grow a beard from then on because of these injuries to his face.

In March 1860, he had the fortunate opportunity of buying one of the houses on the Narutaki estate, the site where he had previously established his Dutch school. He moved into it immediately. Once again, he planted a botanical garden, where he grew plants that he later sent to Holland so that they could be cultivated in his nursery in Leiderdorp.

Siebold was so highly respected that he was one of the few foreigners who could walk about on the streets unarmed. If he was called out to a patient in the middle of the night, all he had to do was have a servant walk ahead of him bearing a white flag with a large 'S' painted on it. This even managed to keep the street thieves at bay.

Life in Edo

By this time, a number of his old students had been promoted to the posts of Imperial Physicians, and they suggested to the shogun that he invite Siebold to Edo to give a series of scientific lectures. The invitation arrived in February 1861, the same month that Siebold's contract with the Trading Company was due to expire. He decided to go to Edo, despite reports from other foreigners that it was unsafe there. The country was in turmoil; Ii Naosuke (1815-1860), a proponent of the opening of Japan, did his best to restore peace but he was murdered in 1860, as were several foreigners. Heusken, who worked as Townsend Harris's interpreter, was killed in 1861, and a few Dutchmen and Russians were also murdered in Yokohama. Siebold was certain that, in addition to his lectures, he would be able to offer some kind of diplomatic assistance in settling some of the conflicts that arose. He was fully aware of the dangers involved and made the following entry in his diary on 13 April, the day before he boarded the ship that was to take him to Yokohama, 'My baggage was put on board the ship this morning, and this afternoon I gave a sealed letter to Mr. Baudin together with a leather letter box for my wife, containing my will, some silver, some pearls and the maps of Ezo and Krafto.' He felt the animosity of the Japanese in Yokohama even more. Alexander von Siebold wrote to his sister stating, 'This city [...] looks like a prison; all the houses are painted black and have fences around them. The streets are completely deserted at night. The few Europeans who are brave enough to go out are armed to the teeth, and remove their pistols and sabres when they enter a house in much the same way as they would take off their hats when coming into ours.' They stayed in the Akabane Palace in Edo, and were provided with a sizeable group of guards, which made them feel as if they were inside a fort. Once again, Siebold started a Dutch school, and each afternoon he gave lessons in medicine and the natural sciences to a large group of scholars. At the same time he also worked on a Japanese-Dutch-English-French dictionary, as well as on the last volumes of *Nippon*, which he had started writing thirty years previously, and which he wished to complete with an essay titled *The creation and foundations of the present constitution.*[17]

He had only been in Edo a few weeks when, one night in July, a gang of *rōnin* attacked the British Embassy under the command of Sir Rutherford Alcock, which was staying only a kilometre away. Four people were killed and nineteen injured in the ensuing fight. Despite the warnings, Siebold only managed to gain access and attend to the injured just before dawn. Almost immediately after this Siebold went to see the State Council, who virtually begged him to use his influence with British politicians to avert a war. The situation had already deteriorated so much that even his diplomatic intervention would have little effect. Siebold took the precaution of increasing the number of guards around his house. Alexander wrote to his mother about this with youthful enthusiasm:

Our house is prepared for war. There are 300 men guarding the palace; five men stand guard in front of our door and another fifteen are posted a short distance away. They all wear armour and carry lances, guns, pikes and sabres. As such, we appear to be safe; still we do not sleep soundly at night when we think of the mangled beds in Tozenji [the British Embassy]. Please do not worry about us though, because we will defend ourselves bravely and we have loyal and brave bodyguards.[18]

Siebold could only add, 'I can hardly write anymore; I am too tired and have not slept for five nights in a row. Do not worry; we shall survive this.' One night an interpreter warned him that an attack was being planned against him, and suggested that he spend the night in a stable – somewhere the *rōnin* would not think of looking for him. It was too much for Siebold, who replied,

'You seem to forget Sir, that I am a Dutch officer. If you wish to run away, then feel free to do so. I will fend off these *rōnin* by myself!'

Siebold is discredited again

Siebold's way of life, his scientific lectures at the Court, his audiences with the shogun and his discussions with Ministers, as well as his role as a negotiator for Holland and many other countries brought him much prestige. However, his political meddling was a cause of great irritation to a number of people. He received orders to return to Yokohama from Consul-General De Witt, the official Dutch envoy, who used the excuse that it was too dangerous for him to remain in Edo. It was actually a difference of opinions regarding the ports which had to be opened-up that brought the situation to a head. Holland, as well as various other foreign powers, wanted all the ports that had been specified in the treaty to be made accessible to them. Siebold advised the shogun that he should only make Nagasaki a free port; all the merchants from the rest of Japan would converge there, thus minimising the obvious threat that foreigners posed to the country. It was clear that Siebold's conflicting opinions would only cause problems between Holland and other world governments, and De Witt informed him that he would no longer be guaranteed Dutch protection if he remained in Edo. Siebold replied that he was not impressed. De Witt was furious and took other measures. He contacted the Japanese government and pressurised them to send Siebold away so as to avoid conflict with the Dutch government. His request came at a time when Siebold's activities had again aroused suspicions among the Japanese. Mise Shūzō, Siebold's companion, had translated a number of Japanese historical and legal texts, a discreditable act that resulted in Shūzō ending up in prison.

The Japanese government asked Siebold to leave Edo on 31 October 1861. He was severely shocked by the fact that the Japanese were sending him away again, especially as he was convinced that he could achieve a great deal on behalf of Dutch interests. Sir Rutherford Alcock had offered his son Alexander, now fifteen years old, work as an interpreter at the British legation, and Siebold eventually agreed to let him stay with the hope that he might continue with his work. Siebold did not cease meddling in politics even after his return to Nagasaki.

The Dutch Minister of Colonies, Loudon, thought that Siebold's tactless activities had to be brought to an end. He ordered Siebold to leave Japan and to work as an advisor in close proximity to Baron Sloet van der Beele (1806-1890), the Governor-General of the Dutch East Indies. The alternative was an honorary discharge from the public service. Siebold left Nagasaki and went to Batavia at the end of April 1862. Obstinate as he was, he thought he could still influence the policies towards Japan from here, and immediately after his arrival he drafted a plan in which he assigned himself the role of Dutch envoy. He would be based in Edo and concerned with the propagation of the Dutch language and the continuation of the tradition of the Dutch school. It was only from a basis of trust, a privilege that Siebold thought was reserved for The Netherlands, that Dutch trade could be re-established and increased.

However, before this plan was even discussed, he received news of a Royal decree issued on 23 July 1862, transferring all responsibilities for Chinese and Japanese affairs from the Ministry of the Colonies to the Ministry of External Affairs. There was little left for Siebold to do after this, so he left Batavia and returned to Holland. He was discharged, at his own request, from the Dutch public service on 7 October 1863, forty years after he had started working for it. It was highly possible that the Dutch government had misled Siebold about his opportunities in Batavia, but the blame did not rest entirely with them. His sympathetic attitude towards Japan and Russia did not always conform to the interests of the Dutch State, and conflicts were inevitable. Siebold was also a difficult person to deal with, and he was acutely aware of his own superiority. His brother-in-law, Karl von Gagern also had this opinion of him and once wrote in a letter, 'Siebold is keen to help and serve but, if I may say so, he displays an extremely exclusive egoism in his helpfulness. In other words, when he helps he wants to do so on his own, especially when it comes to Japanese affairs.'

Siebold left Holland angry and disillusioned, and went to live in Bonn, which was not to his liking either. He eventually moved back to Würzburg to continue his scientific work, but he was hampered by a shortage of funds and the fact that he had left many of his books and manuscripts in Japan, expecting to return there. He continued to correspond with many of his Japanese associates, and was sent material by his son Alexander. He also maintained contact with Russia and other world powers, always with the same goals in mind: to ensure that foreign interaction with Japan progressed as peacefully as possible, and that somehow he could create an opportunity which would enable him to return to his beloved Japan; alas to no avail.

After a few years of unsuccessful lobbying, he travelled to Munich, where he concentrated on organising, displaying and describing the collection of objects he had accumulated during his second trip to Japan. This tiring work in the cold exhibition space became too much for him and he caught a dreadful cold. Shortly after this, he got blood poisoning, and his exhausted body could not resist it. He died on 18 October 1866. His last words were: 'I am going to a beautiful place, a place of peace.'

63. *Siebold, at an advanced age, taken from* Nippon.

58. *Siebold's signature.*

65. *Memorial plaque on the Sieboldhuis. Siebold lived here until 1840, and eventually sold the house in 1847 to the then current tenant Professor Reinwardt.*

66. *Death notice in the* Leidsch Dagblad *on 25 October 1866. (Archive, Leidsch Dagblad).*

67. Camellia japonica;
*related to the tea plant that
Siebold successfully
introduced to Java, taken from
the* Flora Japonica.

The Siebold collections

The number of botanical, zoological and ethnographical objects Siebold brought together during his two visits to Japan and in Europe over a period of forty years runs into the tens of thousands. These collections are still almost complete and kept primarily in Holland and Germany, where Siebold was born, while a number of items ended up in Russia and England. Siebold's sons, Heinrich and Alexander also brought together collections of a similar magnitude, most of which ended up in Austria, and even Japan, where Siebold has a prominent place in the history books as one of the most famous foreigners.

An overview of the collections brought together by Philipp Franz von Siebold is included below. These can mostly be viewed in Leiden and Munich. A small part, which is preserved in Vienna, is not discussed here. The greatest part of the collection Siebold acquired during his first trip to Japan can be found in Leiden. While most of the objects he accumulated during his second trip to Japan (1859-1862) ended up in Munich, a few of them were incorporated into his sons' collections, and are kept in Vienna.

The Leiden collections

The botanical collection

Siebold had two books with him in his luggage when he arrived in Japan in 1823, and these served as the basis of his botanical research. One was *Amoeniates exoticae*, published in 1712 by the German doctor Engelbert Kaempfer (1651-1716), in which he expounded on his experiences, and the observations he had made during his travels through Persia and India. Kaempfer had worked as a doctor on Deshima from 1690 to 1692 and his book included a chapter on Japanese botany, in which he described 517 Japanese plants. The other, more important book was the *Flora Japonica* published in 1784 by Carl Peter Thunberg (1743-1828), a Swedish physician who worked at the trading post on Deshima from 1775 to 1779. This book contained descriptions of 812 different plant species, more than 300 of which could be considered as new to science. According to Siebold, these two books described two-thirds of the Japanese flora, and he greatly respected these two scientists – something he made quite apparent by placing a special memorial plaque to them in his botanical garden on Deshima. It can still be seen in the present-day Deshima Park in Nagasaki.

68. Betula platyphylla; *a
wood sample painted by
Mogami Tokunai. The reverse
side contains a text by Siebold
noting that these trees grow
up to 30 or 40 foot high, and
that the wood is used by the
local inhabitants as packing
material and for water scoops.
(National Herbarium, Leiden).*

69. Phellodendron
amurense; *a wood sample
painted by Mogami Tokunai.
Siebold recorded in* Nippon
*that people eat the fruit of this
tree, and that the bark is used
as roofing material. (National
Herbarium, Leiden).*

70. Quercus serrata; *a wood
sample prepared by Mogami
Tokunai. (National
Herbarium, Leiden).*

Naturally, Siebold set himself the task of completing the work these two men
had started, and he also renamed many of the plants and trees that Thunberg
had described. He was assisted in this by a number of people, only a few of
who are mentioned here: Kō Ryōsai (1799-1846), a young doctor and one of his
most enthusiastic pupils, who had a great interest in botany, and accompanied
Siebold on the court journey. Siebold was to entrust the education of his
daughter Oine, to Kō Ryōsai when he was forced to leave Japan in 1829. The
painter Kawahara Keiga, who was also known as Toyosuke (1786 [?] – after
1859) played an important role in Siebold's research too. Keiga had been
trained to make naturalistic illustrations of foreign imports for the authorities
in Nagasaki, and he put his skills to work for Siebold and others, making
extremely precise drawings of many types of plants. Keiga later learnt the
finer points of European draughtsmanship from the Swiss, C.H. de
Villeneuve, who came to Deshima to help Siebold in 1825. Many of the
illustrations for the *Flora Japonica* were based on Keiga's drawings. Siebold was
also assisted by Itō Keisuke (Itō Keiske) (1803-1901), a doctor from Nagoya,
who later studied botany under Mizutani Hobun. Keisuke went to Nagasaki in
1826 and accompanied Siebold on the court journey. Like his tutor, Keisuke
was also to become Siebold's apprentice, and he was captivated by European
botany and the Linnaean system of plant classification, which he subsequently
promulgated throughout Japan. He even translated Thunberg's book into
Japanese. Siebold learnt a great deal about Japanese botany from Keisuke, who
kept supplying him with new plants together with their Japanese and Chinese

71. *The Siebold Memorial Garden in the botanical gardens at Leiden University. (Carla Teune, Hortus Botanicus, Leiden)*

72. *Orangery in the botanical gardens in Leiden with the creepers,* Akebia quinata *en* Chaenomeles speciosa, *that Siebold brought with him from Japan.*

73. Pinus koraiensis, *taken from the* Flora Japonica.

74. Akebia quinata. *The example that Siebold brought with him can still be seen in the botanical gardens at Leiden University (see ill. 72), taken from the* Flora Japonica.

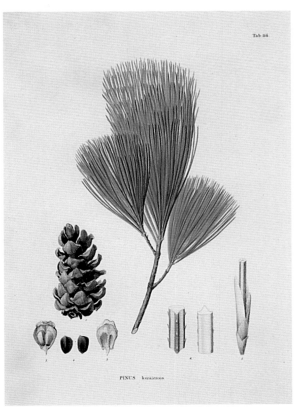

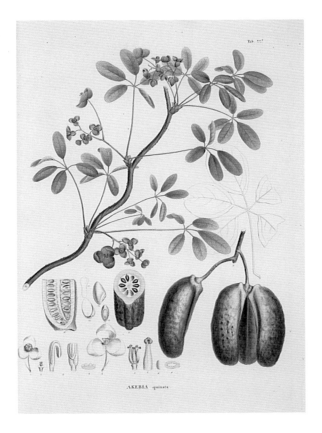

75. Hydrangea otaksa;
Siebold named this plant after his Japanese wife, taken from the Flora Japonica.

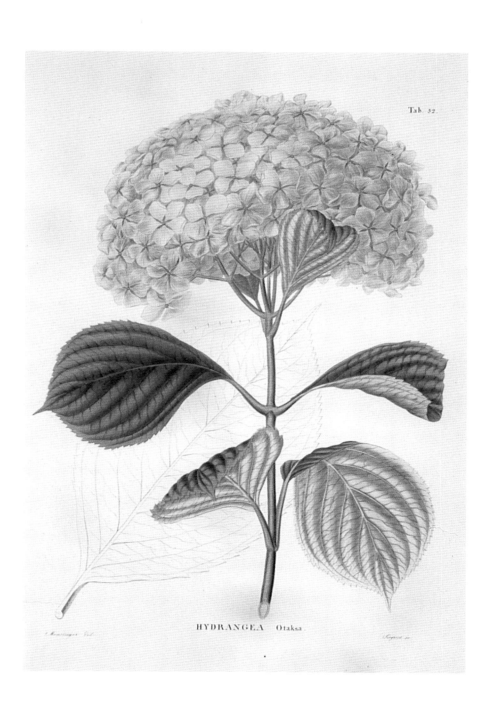

HYDRANGEA Otaksa.

names, which Siebold then researched and identified. Fourteen albums of botanical varieties collected by Keisuke are kept in the National Herbarium, bound in beautiful orange covers. Mogami Tokunai (1755-1836), a geographer and ethnographer, supplied Siebold with important information about the Ainu, as well as maps of the island of Sachalin, something he was not punished for later, despite the fact that it was a major transgression. Many assume that this was because he was so old, and had made such significant scientific contributions to Japan. He gave Siebold a beautiful collection of wood samples, decorated with paintings of the leaves of the respective trees. These are now preserved in the National Herbarium in Leiden.

Heinrich Bürger (1804-1858), a chemist who was sent to Deshima in 1825 in order to assist Siebold, also contributed to his botanical studies. Bürger assumed Siebold's responsibilities as a doctor and researcher after he was banished from Japan in 1829, and continued to send many plants and preserved plant specimens to Holland up until his own departure in 1834. Eighteen different plant varieties have been named after him in recognition of his services to science. The largest proportion of the more than ten thousand plant specimens thus accumulated has been preserved in the National Herbarium. Most of these are dried specimens, although some have also been preserved in formalin.

Siebold sent many live plants to Holland while he was in Japan, and fifteen of these are still growing at the botanical gardens at Leiden University. There are three exquisite wisteria plants growing over a long pergola, which produce a spectacular sea of flowers during the summer. *Akebia quinata* and *Chaenomeles speciosa* have beaten a sinuous path to the top of the orangery; their gnarled stems are proof of their great age. The giant zelkova's and the *Aesculus turbinata* (a sort of horse chestnut) that Siebold personally sent to Leiden still look remarkably healthy and majestic. In addition there are a large number of trees, shrubs and herbs descended from Siebold's original collection, which can now be found in the special Siebold Memorial Garden at the botanical gardens, as can a bust of him that was placed there in 1932. Although many people are unaware of it, a large number of well-known contemporary decorative and garden plants, like the wisteria, hydrangea, camellia, mulberry and peony-rose and many more besides, are now to be found in Europe because of Siebold's activities.

Flora Japonica

75a. Title-page of the
Flora Japonica.

Siebold had not even been on Deshima for a year when he decided to write a *Flora Japonica*. He met the botanist, Joseph Gerhard Zuccarini (1797-1848), a professor at the University of Munich, a few years after he returned to Holland in 1830, and asked him to collaborate with him on the *Flora* and other botanical works. The book would contain beautiful colour plates, which he would use to propagate Japanese (garden) plants in the West. The first volume consisted of twenty issues, each containing five illustrations and an explanatory text. Zuccarini supplied botanical descriptions in Latin; Siebold, the Japanese and Chinese names, plus a description of where each of them grew, their medicinal or economic uses, cultivation techniques and history, all in French. It was these ethnobotanical commentaries by Siebold that were to make the *Flora Japonica* such a valuable work.

The first issue appeared in 1835, and the first volume was completed in 1841. Siebold had sent 250 plants to the botanical gardens in Ghent during his first visit to Japan, and he had been unable to retrieve them since 1830 due to political unrest. However, 65 of these plants were returned to him in 1841, and this gave significant impetus to their research. Unfortunately, Siebold ran into some financial difficulties soon after the publication of the fifth issue of the second volume in 1844, and subsequent issues were delayed. Zuccarini died in 1848, which effectively brought the project to a standstill.

Friedrich Anton Miquel (1811-1871), who had been the director of the National Herbarium since 1862, was extremely interested in Siebold's work, and published the remaining five issues in 1870, several years after Siebold's death in 1866. Miquel discovered many new species in Siebold's collection, and a substantial number of these were dedicated to Siebold and his colleagues. Miquel died in 1871 and work on the project ceased. It has still not been completed.

The *Flora Japonica* was not cheap. Each issue cost 7,5 guilders, which is why a black-and-white edition was made available for half the price. However, it was the beautiful coloured plates, together with the precise botanical descriptions and extremely informative ethnobotanical commentaries that made the *Flora Japonica* such a unique and invaluable botanical reference work.

76. Canis familiaris
japonicus, *taken from the*
Fauna Japonica.

77. Halliaëtos pelagicus major, *taken from the* Fauna Japonica.

The zoological collection

Not much was known about the fauna in Japan when Siebold arrived there. Kaempfer had included a chapter in his *History of Japan* (1727), which was dedicated to land- and aquatic animals, but had only noted their European or Japanese names, with an occasional local anecdote about the usefulness of some of them. Thunberg's researches were somewhat more comprehensive; not only did he compile a list of the animals, but he also collected some examples of a number of different species, which he sent to Europe so that various researchers could work with them.

It was only during the time of Siebold and his assistant Heinrich Bürger that proper research into Japanese fauna actually began. Siebold was fortunate in that previous collectors had paved the road before him, and he was able to release his first publication dedicated to this field as early as 1824. It was based on a collection of natural historical objects (later acquired by the Society of Natura Artis Magistra, in Amsterdam) that had been accumulated by the previous *Opperhoofd*, Jan Cock Blomhoff, during his stay in Japan. Above all, Siebold also enjoyed the freedom he had been granted to collect material in and around Nagasaki and the court journey obviously provided him with many more research opportunities. He could make more excursions, and several of his students, who accompanied him on these trips, were highly motivated and only too keen to track down many different animals for him. His fellow travellers, as well as the people he encountered on the journey, brought him an endless array of birds, reptiles, amphibians, mammals and crustaceans.

At that time, Coenraad Jacob Temminck (1778-1858) was the first director of the National Museum of Natural History in Leiden, which had been established by Willem I in 1820. Temminck, the son of a wealthy Amsterdam merchant, had an enormous collection of birds that he was prepared to donate to the newly established museum on the condition that he was appointed as its director, which duly occurred. He was an avid ornithologist and Siebold considered him the most appropriate person, together with some of his staff, to document the zoological material from Japan. Siebold had already written a letter in 1824, while he was still in Japan, requesting Temminck to write a *Fauna Japonica*, which he agreed to do.

Siebold was to send four large consignments of material. Temminck was not really enthusiastic about the first shipment, which he received in May 1827. His annual report of the same year contained the following description of the collection, 'The only thing we have received so far from Mr. Siebold in Japan is a rather insignificant collection of birds, although it is said that this gentleman has accumulated some important collections in that rarely visited part of the world.'

Temminck's comments on the other shipments are not known. The third of these, sent early in 1829, was the largest and consisted of the 89 crates which had been loaded onto the *Cornelis Houtman*. This was the ship that ran aground in the harbour at Nagasaki during a terrible storm, which eventually led to the 'Siebold incident'. The shipment did eventually arrive in Holland, however. Siebold ended up travelling with the final consignment at the end of 1829, which even included a few live animals, including a monkey, two dogs, a *tanuki* (racoon) and a pair of giant salamanders.

Heinrich Bürger took over Siebold's post when he left Japan, and he also continued to collect objects. Bürger sent another three collections to Holland, the first of which made Temminck extremely enthusiastic. His annual report of 1831 contains the following remarks, 'The receipt of an impressive number of natural historical objects from Mr Bürger in Japan, consisting mainly of fish, is a suitable addition to the earlier collections accumulated by Mr Siebold. It is, in all aspects, a great contribution to the knowledge of the seas of that country, about which we know so little.' Bürger's collections were of such high quality, and so important to Siebold's work, that he received a knighthood in the Order of the Dutch Lion in 1834, in recognition of his services.

In essence, Siebold and Bürger collected and supplied the material and Temminck and his colleagues wrote the text for the *Fauna Japonica*. Five volumes were published between 1833 and 1850. Temminck wrote the texts for the one that dealt with mammals, and co-authored the texts for the volumes about birds, reptiles (and amphibians) and fish with Hermann Schlegel, curator of vertebrate animals, and the second director, after Temminck, of the Museum of Natural History. Wilhem de Haan, the curator of invertebrate animals, wrote the volume about crustaceans. In fact, Siebold was really only the general editor of the complete work, and he wrote the introductions to the two volumes that dealt with reptiles and crustaceans respectively. It was typical of Siebold's character that he later referred to Temminck as his co-author of the *Fauna Japonica* in a letter to the Dutch government. An incomplete manuscript about starfish, sea urchins and related crustaceans with a carapace that was started by J.A. Herklots and included a few illustrations, remains unpublished and is kept in the museum. This work, like the *Flora Japonica* and *Nippon*, was never really completed.

The National Museum of Natural History in Leiden, which was renamed 'Naturalis' contains a considerable portion of both Siebold's and Bürger's zoological collections, varying from stuffed animals, animals or parts of animals preserved in formalin, pictures and illustrations from the *Flora Japonica*, and other works. Additionally, a large part of their mineralogical collection is also stored here. This was mostly accumulated by Bürger who, as a chemist, had more insight into this field. This collection was recently catalogued and a book about it has been published in Japan.

Siebold & Co.

The fact that he established 'The Society for the Import and Cultivation of Japanese Plants in the Netherlands' in 1839 can also be taken as an indication that scientific motives were not the only basis for Siebold's obsessive collecting. He established this society together with the German, Karl Ludwig Blume (1796-1862), the first director of the National Herbarium in Leiden. Blume had also been the director of *'s Lands Plantentuin*, the botanical gardens at Buitenzorg on Batavia from 1822 to 1826. During this period Siebold had sent him all sorts of plants from Japan, which were to be propagated at Buitenzorg. Once back in Holland, the two men decided to stimulate the cultivation of the decorative plants from China and Japan that delighted them so much. They managed to convince the Minister of Colonies to send Dr. Jacques Pierot, an expert on herbs, to Buitenzorg at the government's expense. He helped with the collection and cultivation of the different plants, and organised their transportation to Holland. Once in Holland, the plants would be propagated at Siebold's estate 'Nippon', in Leiderdorp. Diard, the director of Buitenzorg, convinced the Minister that in addition to supplying Siebold and Blume with plants, Pierot would also send them to other scientific parties, including the Academic Gardens in Leiden and Utrecht, and Buitenzorg itself. Diard returned to Europe, and his successor displayed little interest in the garden at Buitenzorg, which gave Pierot more time to fulfil Siebold's and Blume's personal requirements. Moreover, the 'Society' had meantime been changed into a 'The Royal Dutch Company for the Promotion of Horticulture.' This resulted in one angry critic, who viewed the commercial activities of the garden at Buitenzorg with disapproval, describing the two men as follows: 'Messrs. Siebold and Blume, now enjoying Royal protection, started to feel increasingly more powerful, and their behaviour became more impertinent by the day.' He thought they were going too far when they sent a list to the Governor-General containing the names of plants 'presently in *'s Lands Plantentuin*, whose prompt cultivation in Holland was most desirable,' with the request to ensure that 'these plants, which we will require ourselves, not be made available to anybody else for several years.' Not only did they have the audacity to make such a request but, much to this critic's dismay, it was granted too. Pierot was to send 385 Javanese- and 86 Japanese varieties to Holland. Only 60 Javanese- and 17 Japanese plants survived the trip. Pierot died in 1841 while travelling to Japan. He was succeeded in 1843 by Carl Julius Textor, who sent 333 plant species and varieties, and more than 500 plants and bulbs from Deshima to Holland, together with several hundred seeds. Again, only a few survived.

According to Siebold, a total of 733 plant species, and about 400 different types of seeds were sent to Holland from 1829 to 1844. Two hundred and thirty-one plants survived the voyage, and of these 204 would eventually stay alive. He was able to cultivate thirteen varieties from the seeds. The total cost of this enterprise amounted to 14,000 guilders, or 60 guilders per plant.

78. Illicium religiosum, *taken from the* Flora Japonica.

79. Lilium speciosum; *Siebold was also responsible for introducing this distinctive plant to Europe, taken from the* Flora Japonica.

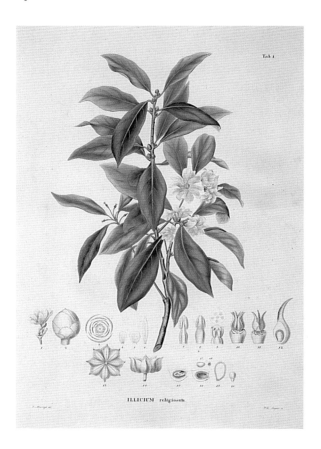

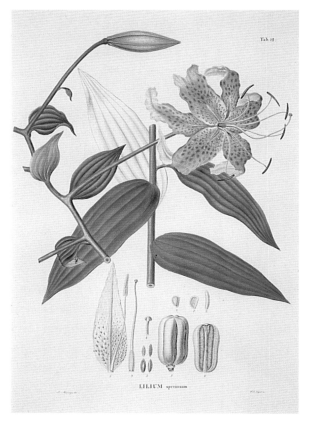

The ethnographic collection

The ethnographic collection of more than 5000 objects is kept at the National Museum of Ethnology in Leiden. The King had already bought Siebold's collection in 1831, but Siebold had been granted full access to it as reference material while he was writing his great dissertation on Japan. It was known as 'The Siebold Collection' from that moment on. Siebold first exhibited his ethnographic collection in 1832 in the house he had recently rented on the Rapenburg, which he opened to the public almost immediately. Many dignitaries from all over Europe visited his museum, including the Dutch King, Willem II (1792-1849) and the future Russian tsar, Alexander II (1818-1881). Many scholars and interested people seemed to be full of admiration for his substantial collection of Japanese objects. Major General Ludwig Freiherr von Welden made the following observations in a German botanical magazine in 1835:

> *There is probably nothing comparable to what is exhibited in the three rooms containing the systematically exhibited treasures which Mr. Von Siebold brought from Japan. One is transferred among all inventions, customs, habits, the art, science and industry of a population which was, until recently, as unknown as man on the moon. From the toiletries of ladies, one enters into the studio of the artisan, from the golden pagoda and schools into an armoury and, as to leave out nothing, whole streets in miniature with their wares, temples for their gods, and houses of pleasure are exhibited. They have been made over there by the Japanese themselves, which is a great safeguard for their authenticity, since there are no artisans or copyists more faithful than the Japanese, which can be seen very well from the likeness of well-known portraits which they copied. For whom all these model representations wouldn't suffice, he will find what he still could wish for in an endless series of drawings and paintings: battles, races and processions are represented in large scrolls which unroll piece for piece for one's eyes. A separate room contains a Japanese library, school- and law books; mathematical treatises, largely illustrated, fill up these publications. A fourth room, finally, is filled with a collection of Japanese clothing, weapons and utensils which Dr. Von Siebold brought from Russia which differ considerably from those areas the traveller visited himself [sic].*[19]

Shortly after Siebold bought the house in 1836, he rented the ground floor (in 1837) to the students' society 'Minerva', which meant that his collection had to be squeezed into the rooms on the first floor. Although the students relocated six years later, the space became even more cramped, because Siebold rented the ground floor and a couple of the upstairs rooms to Professor Caspar G.C. Reinwardt (1773-1854). Reinwardt eventually bought the house in 1847. Siebold, who had meanwhile been living in his house 'Nippon' in Leiderdorp, moved the collection to a building on the Paardensteeg, which was given the name 'Japanese Museum', and was specially arranged as a storage and exhibition space. It was far too small, badly maintained and turned out to be extremely damp, which resulted in some of the collection being damaged or even lost. It was only in 1859 that a more suitable building became available on the more dignified Breestraat. This was mostly thanks to the efforts of Dr. Conradus Leemans (1809-1893), who was the director of the Museum of Antiquities, and who had been the acting director of what was then called 'The National Japanese Museum Von Siebold' at the time of Siebold's second visit to Japan. In time, important additions to the collection here meant that it became more of a general ethnographic museum, and in 1864 it was renamed 'The National Ethnographic Museum'. Its name was changed again in 1937 to 'The National Museum of Ethnology' *(Rijks Ethnographisch Museum)*. The Royal Cabinet of Curiosities in The Hague, which had been established in 1816 by King Willem I, was closed down in 1883. The collections that had been stored here, which had been made by the previous *Opperhoofd* on Deshima, Jan Cock Blomhoff, and Johannes Frederik van Overmeer Fisscher, a former Warehouse Master on the island, were added to Siebold's collection. This meant that the three oldest collections of Japanese objects in Europe were finally gathered together under one roof.

80. Small, white Hirado-porcelain dish shaped like lotus leaves with a crab. (National Museum of Ethnology, Leiden).

81. Bamboo vase used during tea ceremonies. (National Museum of Ethnology, Leiden).

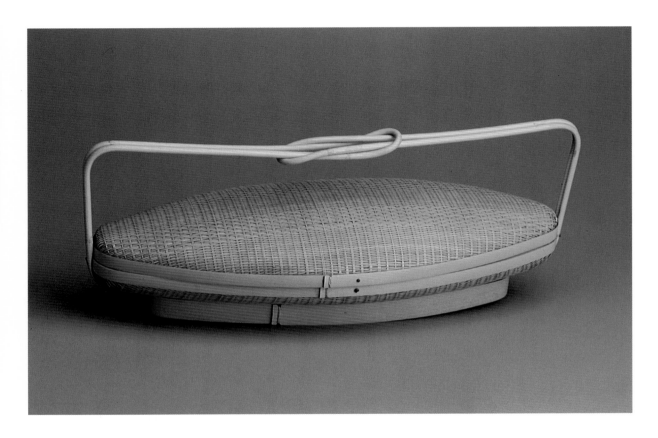

82. *A basket made from woven bamboo, used for serving food. Also depicted in* Nippon. *(National Museum of Ethnology, Leiden).*

83. *Small dish. Hirado-porcelain, with a picture of a courtesan. (National Museum of Ethnology, Leiden).*

The Munich collection

Siebold accumulated another collection during his second trip to Japan, which lasted from August 1859 until the end of April 1862. It was organised according to a system he had developed earlier and had applied to the Leiden collection. It consisted of about 200 books, a number of prints, almost 200 paintings, more than 200 coins from Japan, China, Korea, Siam and the Ryūkyū Islands, weights and measures, medical instruments, religious objects including statues, musical instruments and games. The rest of this collection, which consisted of a total of nearly 2500 objects, was made up of different botanical specimens, minerals, examples of different qualities of silk, cotton and paper, examples of lacquerwork, cabinetwork, turnery, porcelain, pottery, clothing and weapons. Accumulating this collection must rightly be considered a great work of art in itself, especially when its scope, quality and variety are taken into consideration. It is also important to remember that after his arrival in Nagasaki at the beginning of August 1859, Siebold first stayed with Donker Curtius for a short time, moved to a temple in Nagasaki in September, and then bought a house at Narutaki in the middle of 1860, where he started another garden. He travelled by ship to Yokohama in mid-April 1861 and remained in Edo until the spring of 1862. He had very little freedom to move around in Edo because of the hostility that was being openly displayed to foreigners at the time, and returned to Batavia in April that year. He only managed to leave Edo once – from 27 August to 18 September – in order to make a short trip to Yokohama because he was unwell. Despite this, the objects he acquired came from different regions: brushes, ink-cakes and lacquerwork from Kyūshū Island (the place where Nagasaki is situated), the best quality tobacco from Satsuma, finely cut tobacco from Chikusen, tobacco leaves from the Nagasaki area and some exquisite pottery from Takata in Higo Province. He obtained copper ore from Tajima, leatherwork from Muro and Akashi in Harima (two provinces to the north-west of Osaka), bronze from Kyoto, straw basketwork from the area around Nagoya in Owari and bamboo basketwork and lacquerwork from Hakone. A variety of fine objects came from Edo, like a small cabinet, a number of small boxes made from tortoise-shell, varnished ivory carvings, *netsuke* and some bronze vases. He obtained lacquerwork from Mutsu in the north of Japan and even managed to get a few ethnographic objects made by the Ainu, or Ezo on Hokkaido (then called Ezo) and from Sachalin (then called Krafto), including some items of clothing, blue beads known as Krafto *tama*, a watertight box made of straw and a tobacco pouch made of ray skin. Some items bear testimony to the more pleasant times he had in Edo, like the beautiful lacquerwork he received as gifts from the Governor of Kanagawa, from the Councillor of Tsushima, from the Councillor and Minister of Foreign Affairs, the Lord of Yamato, from the Councillors in Edo, from the Governors of Foreign Affairs in Edo, and even a military dress sword *(tachi)* offered to Siebold by the Taikun when he left Edo in 1861. A number of items he received from the Governors of Nagasaki and from his learned friends in Edo appear to have been farewell presents. There are definite similarities between some of these objects and those he obtained thirty years earlier; others were manufactured using the same techniques, but with superior craftsmanship, illustrating the advances that had taken place. Foreign influences can also be seen in some of the more contemporary lacquered goods, like a snuffbox, a cigar box and cigar cases made from papier maché, and a matchbox. It is therefore extremely regrettable that the Dutch government did not buy this collection – they found the price too high and Japanese products were not considered as exclusive as they had been before Japan opened its borders. This collection was only exhibited in Amsterdam in the premises of the Society for National Industry *(Vereeniging voor Volksvlijt)*, accompanied by a printed catalogue titled *A guide for the visitors to the collection of objects of science, art and industry and products of the industry of the Japanese Empire, collected during the period of 1859 to 1862 by Jhr. Ph.F. von Siebold from the Japanese Empire.* [20] The true nature of Siebold's

84. Koro – *an incense pot. (National Museum of Ethnology, Leiden).*

mission – the promotion of trade – was not concealed at all: the subtitle read: *To disseminate knowledge about the country and peoples of Japan, and of products suitable for export trade.* This allowed for statements like: 'The finest grades of porcelain clay, or kaolin, either in it's raw state or pulverised, could conceivably be an export product if it could be included as ballast with a shipment of tea.' Another indication that export trade was already going on is a list of seventeen different types of wood under the heading: *The following types of wood may be considered for the export trade,* with the statement that almost all of 'these types of wood have been imported to the Acclimatisation Gardens of Von Siebold & Co. in Leiden, which can provide young trees.'

When the exhibition ended, Siebold took the collection with him to Würzburg, where he set it up in an assembly hall at a school. The Bavarian government showed an interest in it, so he moved it to Munich in April 1866 and installed it in a museum there. Time would not allow him to participate in the actual sale of the collection. The head curator of the Bavarian scientific collections had informed him in June 1865 that the sale would be finalised in the next budget year. However, this did not happen, nor did it occur in 1867 or 1868, as it was rejected by the Assembly of the Kingdom of Bavaria. It was eventually bought in 1874, and the collection is now housed in the State Museum of Ethnology in Munich.

The scientific value of Siebold's collections

It would take months, if not years, to view all the material that Siebold collected over the forty-year period. At the very least, it is incredible that one person was able to accumulate such a variety of objects in so many different fields. Siebold tried not only to collect as many things as he could, but also to do it as systematically as possible. At the time botanical data was usually organised by implementing the Linnaean system of classification - something Siebold did, much like his predecessor Thunberg.

Ethnology was a totally new field and no methodology had yet been created for it and museology only started to be developed as more museums were established. Initially Siebold only collected natural historical objects: animals, plants and trees, and the materials that were derived from them. He received some of these items from grateful patients and students, and even requested his students to actively collect such items for him. He employed a hunter and a fisherman who collected different animals for him, which he would then have preserved by someone else. Increasingly more objects that were manufactured from animals or natural products started to be included in his collection, usually as examples of the ways in which natural materials from Japan were used. He saw the possibility of considerably increasing and completing his collection during the court journey, and he acquired still more examples of basketwork, lacquerwork, marquetry and such like. It was only after his return that he developed a system to classify this collection. It was primarily based on the raw materials that had been used for their manufacture, whether they were animal or vegetable, and whether they had been used as is or had been processed to change them into useable materials. Siebold gradually developed an eye for ethnographic objects. Like Blomhoff and Fisscher before him, he made ample use of the services provided by the well-known artist, Kawahara Keiga, and his studio, to fulfil his desire to document as much information as possible on the architectural style of the houses, various crafts, diverse clothing, the different races and their physiognomy, eating habits, festive occasions, and more besides. Meticulously detailed drawings were made of tools, bridge constructions, and procedures for dyeing cloth and such like, all with the intention of conveying the most accurate information possible. In this way, the complete collection of ethnographic objects provides a general overview of the Japanese traditions and customs, their daily life and the products they manufactured at the time they were acquired, namely the first half of the 19th century. In a way, the

85. Preparing the wedding feast. Painting by Kawahara Keiga (made between 1825-1829). (National Museum of Ethnology, Leiden).

86. Funeral cortege. Painting by Kawahara Keiga (made between 1825-1829) (National Museum of Ethnology, Leiden).

collection can therefore be considered a veritable time capsule.

The fact that Siebold divided his ethnographic collection into categories, as he did with his botanical one, is probably the reason why it is often considered a scientific collection. Siebold first propounded this system of classification in his treatise *A short synopsis and discussion of the expediency and usefulness of an ethnographic museum in The Netherlands.*[21] He sent this document to the King in 1837, together with his request that the promise to purchase his collection for the country be fulfilled. He specified the categories as follows:

1 – Scientific objects: books, manuscripts, woodblock prints, drawings and paintings, coins and a few antiquities.
2 – Products of culture and industry: which were again separated according to the kind of raw materials and techniques that went into the preparation and manufacture of the various items.
3 – Models of buildings and assorted equipment, and tools used in agriculture, fishing and other domestic work.
4 – Ethnographic objects from the tributary and appended countries of Japan like Ezo, the southern Kurile Islands and the Korean peninsula, as well as objects from Tibet and Siberia.

Of course, the question arises as to what extent Siebold's accumulation of information was actually motivated by science. In fact, Siebold provides the answer to this in the document mentioned above, where he wrote: 'The purpose of the ethnographic museum is to broaden the knowledge of countries and people in general. Such an institution, when established in Holland, should firstly concentrate on Dutch colonies and other countries outside Europe, with which we trade or have some special form of contact […]'. Additionally, his introduction to a catalogue for an exhibition of 'Products of Japan and its industry' *(Japansche voortbrengselen en voorwerpen van nijverheid)* that he organised in Leiden in 1845 stated: 'Research requested by the King into products and objects that might increase the export of such items from Japan to Holland had recently resulted in the arrival of a collection of Japanese products.' (Textor, who had been asked to bring seeds for Siebold's horticultural business, had collected all the products exhibited in 1845 and Siebold added much of this material to his own collection.) A number of remarks about some of the objects also point to commercial motives. He wrote the following about a pot of caviar: 'Japanese caviar exceeds the Russian in taste and purity,' and this about tree-resin: 'As an export item this product deserves a special mention, and is worthy of manufacturers' attention.' Clearly, Siebold was not only aware of the commercial possibilities, but he often researched them in detail. Seen from this perspective, his ethnography was sometimes nothing more than a form of 'educated commercialism,' but it should not be forgotten that this was the reason for sending him to Japan in the first place. Shortly before his trip, the political developments in Europe had resulted in significant reductions in the amount of trade with the colonies and Japan. Siebold's research into the Japanese and their way of life definitely improved trading relationships with that country.

That his collection was intended to eventually become a general ethnographic museum under Leemans's supervision can be concluded from the fact that he also collected objects from the Kurile Islands, Korea, the Ryūkyū Islands, Tibet and other countries. He bought some other collections later, including one from the German, Heinrich C. Macklot (1799-1832), which consisted of objects that had been collected in the eastern part of the Indonesian Archipelago between 1825 and 1832, and he added objects from America, New Zealand, Samoa and Haiti. Siebold was keen to see the Japanese collections of Cock Blomhoff and Van Overmeer Fisscher, previously housed at the Royal Cabinet of Curiosities in The Hague, combined with his. This wish was eventually fulfilled although only after his death in 1883, when the Cabinet was closed down. Introducing these elements of cultural comparison meant that Siebold's collection finally acquired an ethnographic and scientific character.

Epilogue

Deshima is often referred to as a conduit for Western knowledge, which enabled Japan to become part of the Western world in an astonishingly short space of time once it had opened it's borders. Siebold played an irrefutably enormous role in this. On the other hand, he also used this conduit himself, bringing many thousands of plants, seeds, animals, products and implements to the West, including important and sensitive information like geodetic measurements, geographical data and maps.

Siebold had decided early in his career that he wanted to conduct scientific research in distant countries. He originally thought of going to Brazil and became a member of the Senckenberg Natural History Society in Frankfurt, which gave him the task of acquiring a collection of natural historical objects for the recently established museum there. However, intervention by Franz Harbaur, a friend of the family who worked for the Dutch Health Service, resulted in him going to the Dutch East Indies instead. Supported by requests from the Academies of Frankfurt and Vienna to conduct natural historical research, he joined the Dutch civil service and went to Java, where he was to work as a physician for the army.

He must have welcomed the opportunity of subsequently being sent to Japan by Van der Capellen to conduct extensive and cohesive research. More specifically, his tasks included researching Japan's religions, laws, constitution, geography, revenues and taxation, farming methods, customs, arts and sciences, language, natural environment and medicinal herbs. In fact, his assignment was directed more at possible trading opportunities, a job that was made for him, if his remarks concerning this in his various publications and his later activities trading plants and seeds are to be taken as any indication. He had already demonstrated his organisational abilities in the way in which he motivated his students and assistants to help him acquire his collection during his first visit to Japan from 1823 to 1829. He also started to prepare the processing of his collection while still in Japan, and persuaded Temminck to take on the task of writing the *Fauna Japonica*. Many of his other colleagues would also participate in this work: Bürger and De Villeneuve, who assisted Siebold when he was in Japan and after his departure; and Schlegel, De Haan, Zuccarini, Blume, Kuo Ch'êng-chang, Hoffmann, Melvill de Carnbee, De Vriese, etc., in Holland. As such, he did not have to get too deeply involved with projects like the *Flora* and *Fauna Japonica* and, thanks to the efforts of Kuo and Hoffman, was able to include a great number of the translations they made of original Japanese texts in his book *Nippon*.

He initially started writing *Nippon* with great zeal and enthusiasm after his return to Holland, and he spent a year travelling through Europe on a sort of victory tour immediately after the first two volumes were published. However, it seems that he became increasingly more interested in the issue of trade with Japan. His main concern was that Japan should open its borders to the rest of the world in a peaceful manner, and was prepared to give advice whenever it was required. He considered this a necessary part of his duties as an advisor to the Dutch government on Japanese affairs, and he composed a letter to the Japanese government on behalf of King Willem II. He travelled to St. Petersburg after he heard of Russia's intentions to send a convoy of ships to Japan. Nothing specific is known about his contacts with America, but it is certain that Commodore Perry knew of Siebold. No doubt the sections in *Nippon* that dealt with the geography, and more specifically with the seas around Japan, were of great use to him.

It was his nursery at 'Nippon', rather than his collection (which he had seriously neglected), that lured Siebold back to Holland after he started spending winters in Germany from the end of the 1830's on. The international mail-order company that sold plants, seeds and saplings operated from here – partly at the expense of *'s Lands Plantentuin* in Buitenzorg. Leemans organised the collection during Siebold's second trip to Japan, and it was thanks to his energetic and systematic approach that parts of it could be saved and eventually exhibited to the public again.

Siebold tried to get involved in all areas during his second trip to Japan. He started another botanical garden at Narutaki, dabbled in politics, advised the Japanese government to only open the port of Nagasaki to foreign ships, resumed lecturing in Edo – even in international relations – and accumulated a second collection, which was as good as the first.

Still, his unwavering commitment to a peaceful policy towards Japan by the rest of the world, and his plea for a greater understanding of Japan's interests came too late. Too many changes had already taken place, and forces were already at work inside Japan that would eventually lead to greater upheaval than could be caused by the presence of a few foreigners, who were mostly based in Yokohama. It is probably a good thing that Siebold did not have to witness all of this, and hopefully the frustrations he encountered in his life and his work did not prevent him from realising what a privileged position he actually had. He was one of very few foreigners who lived in Japan during a time when it was completely isolated from the rest of the world, and experiencing an economic boom and general prosperity. Thirty years later he was one of the few who were present in Japan when it was still trying to find its place in the world. He may also have been consoled by the fact that his sons were extremely happy and enjoyed the time they spent in Japan – not least because of the reputation of the name 'Siebold'.

Chronology

1796	Philipp Franz von Siebold born on 17 February in Würzburg, Germany.
1815	Starts studying medicine at the University of Würzburg (subjects include chemistry, botany and physics).
1820	Completes his studies in medicine, surgery and anatomy, obtains his doctorate and establishes himself as a physician in Heidingsfeld.
1822	Appointed as Surgeon-Major in the Dutch East-Indies Army on 21 June.
1823	Arrives in Batavia on 13 February and is appointed to the post of physician at the trading post on Deshima on 18 April. He also receives instructions to conduct research into Japanese natural history, laws and politics. Arrives in Deshima on 12 August and starts teaching almost immediately. 'Marries' Kusumoto Sonogi, also known as Otaki (1807-1865).
1824	Starts a botanical garden on Deshima at the request of the government in Batavia. Opens his school in Narutaki, just outside Nagasaki.
1825	Dr. Heinrich Bürger arrives from Batavia to help Siebold with his geological research, accompanied by C.H. de Villeneuve, the illustrator.
1826	Accompanies *Opperhoofd* De Sturler on the court journey to Edo (15 February to 7 July). Bürger, Keiga and several of his Japanese students join the delegation.
1827	The government in Batavia requests his return there, with the possibility that he may have to return to Holland. Von Siebold's daughter Oine (1827-1903) is born.
1828	A severe storm on 18 September causes the ship, with 89 crates containing Siebold's collection, to run aground on the coast at Nagasaki. The discovery of forbidden objects leads to the detainment of Siebold, Takahashi and many others. Siebold is placed under house arrest.
1829	Siebold is subject to lengthy cross-examination and is banished from Japan on 22 October. Siebold leaves Japan on 30 December.
1830	Arrives in Batavia on 18 January and travels on to Holland, where he arrives on 7 July. He meets Dr. Hoffmann in Antwerp, who is later to become the first Professor of Japanese Studies at Leiden University.
1831	King Willem I agrees to buy Siebold's ethnographic collection on 20 April and to pay an initial advance of 12,000 guilders.
1832	Hires the house at 19 Rapenburg, where he organises his collection and opens it to the public. Travels to Germany in the autumn.
1833	Returns to The Netherlands in the summer. Presents the first copy of *Nippon* to the Society of Dutch Letters on 26 November.

1834   Travels to Russia and Germany from mid-1834 to mid 1835. Meets Tsar Nicolas I and scholars like Ritter, Ehrenberg and Von Humboldt.

1835   Travels in Germany and Austria. Meets Zuccarini, and others.

1836   Buys the house at 19 Rapenburg on 22 August.

1837   Rents the ground floor to the Students' Society 'Minerva.' His collection is moved to the first floor.

1838   King Willem I finally buys his ethnographic collection on 1 February for 58,500 guilders. The remaining 42,000 guilders is to be paid as four annual instalments.

1839   From now on he spends his winters in Germany, where he meets his future wife, Helene von Gagern.

1840   Buys a piece of ground in Leiderdorp, where he builds the villa, 'Nippon' and starts a nursery.

1842   Establishes the plant and seed company, Siebold & Co. with Blume and Rodbard.

1843   In November the Ministry of Colonies asks him to write a letter to the Japanese government regarding the international situation.

1844   The letter is delivered to the governor of Nagasaki in July by *Opperhoofd* Pieter Albert Bik

1845   The Student Society 'Minerva' finds another location. Siebold rents his house to Professor Reinwardt. Marries Lady Helene von Gagern (1820-1877) in Berlin on 10 July.

1846   His first son, Alexander (1846-1911) is born.

1847   Buys the Monastery of St. Martin near Boppard am Rhein. Sells his house at 19 Rapenburg to Professor Reinwardt. The collection is transferred to the Paardensteeg.

1848   His daughter Helene (1848-1927) is born.

1850   His daughter Mathilde (1850-1906) is born.

1851   Has contact with America and advises the government about its plans to opening Japanese ports to American ships.

1852   His son Heinrich (1852-1908) is born.

1853   Is invited to St. Petersburg in January to discuss Russian plans regarding the opening of Japanese borders. Sells his house in Boppard in September and moves to Bonn, where he lectures and continues working on *Nippon*.

1854   His son Maximiliaan (1854-1887) is born.

1858   Devises a plan to establish a trading company that will concentrate on Japan and presents it to the Dutch government in the spring. In December he learns that his banishment from Japan has been revoked.

1859   In February he is given the task of presenting the Japanese government

101

with a modified trade agreement between Holland and Japan. Begins preparing for his trip.

Departs on his second trip to Japan from Marseilles on 13 April.

Leemans takes over the administration of the collections and, on 17 July once again opens them to the public in a building on the Breestraat, under the name 'The National Japanese Museum Von Siebold.'.

Arrives in Nagasaki on 4 August.

1860   He buys a house in Narutaki during the summer and starts another nursery there.

1861   He is asked to go to Edo in February and starts staying there in April, resuming his lectures.

He is banished from Edo, and Japan itself, in October.

1862   Leaves Japan at the end of April, stays a few months in Batavia and returns to Europe in November.

1863   Returns to Bonn in January.

Exhibits the collection he brought together during his second trip to Japan in Amsterdam, and offers it to the Dutch government, who find it too expensive.

Leaves the Dutch service on 7 October and receives an annual pension of 4000 guilders.

1864   Moves to Würzburg in the spring.

His first collection is greatly enlarged, and exhibited under the name National Museum of Ethnography in a building on the Hogewoerd.

1865   Travels to Paris in October to discuss Japanese politics.

1866   Transfers his second collection to Munich in the hope that he can sell it there. Arranges an exhibition.

Dies in Munich on 18 October and is buried in the Alten Südlichen graveyard on the Thalkirchner Strasse.

87. Pair of screens presented by the shogun to King Willem II. (National Museum of Ethnology, Leiden).

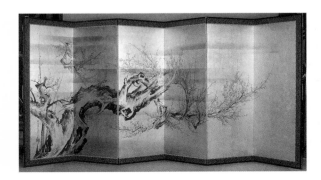 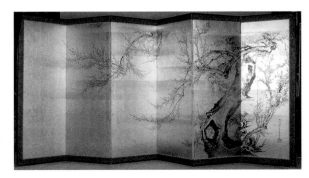

Listed by subject and in chronological order

Siebold bibliography

Natural history

1824 *De historia naturalis in Japonia statu/.../cui accedunt spicilegia faunae japonicae* (Batavia 1824; 2nd ed.: Würzburg 1826; 1827)

1828 'V. Siebolds Nachrichten aus Japan', in: *Flora, oder Botanische Zeitung*, Regensburg 11 (1828) 753-62 (Botanisches Archiv, Leipzig 43 [1942] 517-20)

1829 'Einige Worte über den Zustand der Botanik auf Japan in einem Schreiben an den Praesidenten der Akademie; nebst einer Monographie der Gattung Hydrangea und einigen Proben japanischer Litteratur über die Kräuterkunde, datirt Dezima den 18then December 1825', in: *Nova Acta Physico-Medica Academiae Leopoldino-Carolinae Naturae Curiosorum*, Bonn 14/2 (1829), 671-96

1830 'Synopsis plantarum oeconomicarum universi regni Japonici', in: *Verhandelingen van het Bataviaasch Genootschap van Kunsten en Wetenschappen*, Batavia 12 (1830) i-iv, 1-74

1833 *Fauna Japonica sive descriptio animalium quae in itinere per Japoniam, jussu et auspiciis superiorum, qui summum in India Batava imperium tenent, suscepto, annis 1823-1830 collegit, notis observationibus et adumbrationibus illustravit Ph.Fr. de Siebold.* 5 vols. Leiden 1833-1850 (with C.J. Temminck, H. Schlegel, W. de Haan)

1835 *Flora Japonica, sive plantae, quas in imperio Japonico collegit, descripsit, ex parte in ipsis locis pingendas curavit Dr. Ph.Fr. de Siebold. /...&tc.* Leiden 1835-1841 (with J.G. Zuccarini)

1837 *Erwiederung auf W.H. de Vriese's Abhandlung 'Het gezag van Kaempfer, Thunberg, Linnaeus en anderen omtrent den botanischen oorsprong van den ster-anijs des handels gehandhaafd tegen Dr. Ph.Fr. von Siebold en Prof. J.G. Zuccarini'.* Leiden/Leipzig 1837

1843 'Plantarum, quas in Japonia collegit Dr. Ph. Fr. de Siebold genera nova, notis characteristicis delineationibusque illustrata proponunt Dr. Ph.Fr. de Siebold et Dr. J.G. Zuccarini'. 1, in: *Abhandlungen der mathematisch-physikalischen Classe der Königlich Bayerischen Akademie der Wissenschaften*, München 3 (1843) 717-50

1844 *Kruidkundige naamlijst van oud en nieuw ingevoerde Japansche en Chineesche planten.* Leiden 1844

1844 'Liste des plantes anciennement et nouvellement importées du Japon et de la Chine, cultivées dans la pépinière de la Société Royale pour l'encouragement de l'horticulture, outre quelques éclaircissements historiques sur l'importation de plantes du Japon, depuis l'année 1824 jusqu'en 1844', in: *Annuaire de la Société Royale pour l'encouragement de l'horticulture dans les Pays-Bas* (ed., C.L. Blume and Ph.F. v. Siebold) Leiden 1844, 1-39

1845 'Florae Japonicae familiae naturales, adjectis generum et specierum exemplis selectis. Sectio prima. Plantae Dicotyledoneae polypetalae', in: *Abhandlungen der mathematisch-physikalischen Classe der Königlich Bayerischen Akademie der Wissenschaften*, München 4/2 (1845) 109-204 (with J.G. Zuccarini)

1846   'Florae Japonicae familiae naturales, adjectis generum et specierum exemplis selectis. Sectio altera. Plantarum dicotyledoneae (gamopetalae, monochlamydeae) et monocotyledonae', in: *Abhandlungen der mathematisch-physikalischen Classe der Königlich Bayerischen Akademie der Wissenschaften*, München 4/3 (1846) 123-240 (with J.G. Zuccarini?)

1858   *Annales d'horticulture et de botanique, ou Flore des Jardins du royaume des Pays-Bas, et histoire des plantes cultivées et ornementales les plus intéressantes des possessions Néerlandaises aux Indes Orientales, en Amérique et en Japon, redigée par Ph.Fr. de Siebold et W.H. de Vriese*, 1, Leiden 1858 [ed.]

1863   *Sur l'état de l'horticulture au Japon*. Leiden 1863

1870   *Flora Japonica, sive plantae, quas in imperio Japonico collegit, descripsit, ex parte in ipsis locis pingendas curavit Dr. Ph.Fr. de Siebold*. Volumen Secundum, ab auctoribus inchoatum relictum ad finem perduxit F.A.Guil. Miquel. Leiden, in Siebolds Akklimationsgarten 1870.

Geography

1840   *Karte vom Japanischen Reiche*. Leiden 1840

1843   'Documents importants sur la découverte des îles de Bonin par des navigateurs néerlandais en 1639', in: *Nouvelles annales des voyages et des sciences géographiques*, Paris 98, 4/2 (1843) 318-40

1851   *Atlas von Land- und Seekarten vom Japanischen Reiche*. Berlin 1851

1852   *Geschichte der Entdeckungen im Seegebiete von Japan nebst Erklaerung des Atlas &tc.* Leiden 1852

1854   *Urkundliche Darstellung der Bestrebungen von Niederland und Russland zur Eröffnung Japan's*. Bonn 1854

1858   'Aardrijks- en volkenkundige toelichtingen tot de ontdekkingen van Maerten Gerritsz Vries met het fluitschip Castricum A.o. 1643 in 't Oosten en in 't Noorden van Japan, dienende tot zeemansgids langs de Oostkust van Japan, naar de eilanden Jezo, Krafto en de Kurilen, benevens eene verhandeling over de Ainotaal en de voortbrengselen der Aino-landen', in: *Reize van Maarten Gerritsz. Vries in 1643 naar het Noorden en Oosten van Japan, volgens het Journaal gehouden door C.J. Coen, op het schip Castricum* [...]. Uitgegeven vanwege het Koninklijk Instituut voor taal-, land- en volkenkunde van Nederlandsch Indië, Amsterdam 1858, 263-440 (ook afzonderlijk verschenen, Amsterdam 1858)

1858   'Über Vulkane auf Japan', in: Alexander v. Humboldt, *Kosmos. Entwurf einer physischen Weltbeschreibung*, 4 Stuttgart/Tübingen 1858, 399-402

Medicine

1825   'Beantwoording van eenige vragen over de Japansche vroedkunde, door mijnen leerling Mimazunzo geneesheer tot Nagasaki', in: *Verhandelingen van het*

Bataviaasch Genootschap van Kunsten en Wetenschappen, Batavia 10 (1825) 191-208 (German trans.: Journal für Geburtshilfe, Frauenzimmer- und Kinderkrankheiten, 6/3 [1826] 687-702)

1833   'Iets over de acupunctur (Naaldensteekkunde); getrokken uit eenen brief van den Japansch-Keizerlijken Naaldensteker Isi Saka Sotels', in: *Verhandelingen van het Bataviaasch Genootschap van Kunsten en Wetenschappen*, Batavia 14 (1833) 378-89

1855   'Geschichtliche Übersicht der Einführung und Entwicklung der Arzneiwissenschaft in Japan, vom 24.11.1854', in: *Verhandlungen des naturhistorischen Vereins der preussischen Rheinlande und Westphalens*, Bonn 12 (1855) xvii-xxiii

Language

1826   'Epitome linguae japonicae. Cum tabulis IX xylographicis, in ipsa Japonia incisis', in: *Verhandelingen van het Bataviaasch Genootschap van Kunsten en Wetenschappen*, Batavia 11 (1826) 63-136 (2nd ed.: Leiden 1863)

Collections and catalogues

1833   *Bibliotheca Japonica, sive selecta quaedam opera Sinico-Japonica in usum eorum, qui literis Japonicis vacant*. 6 vols. Leiden 1833-1841 (with J. Hoffmann)

1845   *Catalogus librorum et manuscriptorum Japaonicorum*. Leiden 1845 (with J. Hoffmann)

1862   *Catalogue de la bibliothèque apportée au Japon*. Deshima 1862

General

1833   *Nippon. Archiv zur Beschreibung von Japan und dessen Neben- und Schutzländern: Jezo mit den südlichen Kurilen, Krafto, Kooraï und den Liukiu-Inseln, nach japanischen und europäischen Schriften und eigenen Beobachtungen bearbeitet*. Leiden 1832-58 (Dutch, French and Russian translations)

Ethnology

1831   'Moeurs et usages des Ainos', in: *Nouveau Journal Asiatique*, Paris 7 (1831) 73-80

1832   'Verhandeling over de afkomst der Japaners', in: *Verhandelingen van het Bataviaasch Genootschap van Kunsten en Wetenschappen*, Batavia 13 (1832) 183-275

Etnographic collection

1843   *Lettre sur l'utitilité des musées ethnographiques et sur l'importance de leur création dans les états européens, qui possèdent des colonies, ou qui entretiennent des relations commerciales avec les autres parties du monde, à M. Edmé-François Jomard, Conservateur-Administrateur du Dépôt Géographique de la Bibliothèque Royale*. Paris 1843

1845   *Tentoonstelling van Japansche voortbrengselen en voorwerpen van nijverheid, op last*
        van Z.M. den Koning, ten voordele van de armen der stad Leyden. Leiden 1845

1863   *Handleiding bij het bezigtigen der verzameling van voorwerpen van wetenschap, kunst*
        en nijverheid en voortbrengselen van het Rijk Japan, bijeengebracht gedurende de jaren
        1859 tot 1862 door Jhr. Ph.F. von Siebold, en tentoongesteld in het lokaal der
        Vereeniging voor Volksvlijt te Amsterdam. Ter verspreiding van de kennis van Land- en
        Volkenkunde en van voorwerpen geschikt voor den Uitvoerhandel. Amsterdam 1863

Politics

1861   *Open brieven uit Japan.* Deshima 1861

1861   'Das Attentat auf die englische Gesandtschaft in Yeddo. Von einem historisch-
        politischen Gesichtspuncte betrachtet', in: *Kölnische Zeitung* 307 (5.11.1861)

1864   'Rundschau am politischen Horizont des Sonnenaufgang-Landes Nippon
        (Japan)', in: *Allgemeine Zeitung*, Augsburg, Beilage 288 (14.10.1864); 289
        (15.10.1864); 297 (23.10.1864); 298 (24.10.1864); 299 (25.10.1864); 304 (30.10.1864);
        308 (3.11.1864); 328 (23.11.1864); 330 (25.11.1864); 336 (1.12.1864); 342 (7.12.1864);
        352 (17.12.1864); 4 (4.1.1865)

Various

1836   *Japanische Weisen* [...] *für das Piano eingerichtet.* Leiden 1836 (2nd ed.: Wien 1874)

1846   Le moniteur des Indes-Orientales et Occidentales. Recueil de mémoires et de
        notices scientifiques et industriels, de nouvelles et de faits importants
        concernant les possessions Néerlandaises d'Asie et de'Amerique. Avec la
        coopération de plusieurs membres de la Société des Arts et des Sciences de
        Batavia, par Ph.Fr. de Siebold et P. Melvill de Carnbee, 1, Den Haag/Batavia
        1846/47 [ed.]

Notes

1. *Nippon. Archiv zur Beschreibung von Japan und dessen Neben- und Schutzländern Jezo mit den südlichen Kurilen, Sachalin, Korea und den Liukiu Inseln von Ph.Fr. von Siebold herausgegeben von seinen Söhnen.* Würzburg und Leipzig, 1897, p. XVI.

2. Philipp Franz von Siebold will be referred to as Siebold from here on.

3. Körner, Hans, 'Siebold. Beitrage zur Familiengeschichte' in: *Die Würzburger Siebold. Eine Gelehrtenfamilie des 18. Und 19. Jahrhunderts.* (Deutsches Familienarchiv. Ein genealogisches Sammelwerk, Band 34/35), Neustadt a/d Aisch 1967, p. 360.

4. Coningh, C.T. van Assendelft de, *Mijn verblijf in Japan*, Amsterdam 1856, pp 19f.

5. Brinkhorst, Laurens Jan, 'Nederlanders en Japan: verleden en toekomst.' in: *In het spoor van de Liefde. Japans-Nederlandse ontmoetingen sinds 1600.* Amsterdam, 1986, p. 7.

6. At the beginning of the 19th century, the Dutch language was referred to as 'Low German'.

7. Kure Shūzō, *Philipp Franz von Siebold. Leben und Werk.* München, 1996, p. 60.

8. Beantwoording van eenige vragen over de Japanse vroedkunde door mijnen leerling Mimazunzo [Mima Junzō] geneesheer te Nagasaki, aangeboden aan het Bataviaasch Genootschap van Kunsten en Wetenschappen, door den Med. Dr. Siebold, (1825).

9. The *daimyō* were obliged to stay alternatively in their own domains or in the capital, Edo. Tokugawa Ieyasu proclaimed this highly efficient rule at the beginning of the 17th century in order to guarantee his hegemony. This law, known as *sankin kōtai*, also ruled that they had to leave their families in Edo at all times, effectively as the Shōgun's hostages.

10. Körner, p. 385.

11. 'Iets over de acupunctuur (Naaldensteekkunde); getrokken uit eenen brief van den Japansch-Keizerlijken Naaldensteker Isi Saka Sotels' in the *Verhandelingen van het Bataviaasch Genootschap van Kunsten en Wetenschappen.*

12. *Nippon*, p. XX.

13. Körner, p. 405.

14. Körner, p. 416.

15. *Archief voor de beschrijving van Japan en deszelfs toegevoegde en cijnsbare landen: Jezo met de zuidelijke Kurilen, Krafto, Kooraï en de Liukiu-eilanden, volgens Japansche en Europische geschr*iften

en eigene waarneming bewerkt.

16. Körner, p. 448.

17. Die Entstehung und Begrundung der gegenwärtigen Staatsform.

18. *Flora Japonica*, 18 (14 November) 1835, pp. 668f

19. Forrer, M., 'The Leiden collections of Philipp Franz von Siebold', in: *Die Japansammlungen Philipp Franz und Heinrich von Siebold*. Miscellanea 12. Tokyo, 1996, pp. 15-33.

20. Handleiding bij het bezigtigen der verzameling van voorwerpen van wetenschap, kunst en nijverheid en voortbrengselen van het Rijk Japan, bijeengebracht gedurende de jaren 1859 tot 1862, door Jhr. Ph. F. von Siebold.

21. Kort begrip en ontwikkeling van de doelmatigheid en van het nut van een ethnographisch museum in Nederland.

Beukers, H., *The mission of Hippocrates in Japan. Philipp Franz von Siebold in his role as medical doctor.* Amsterdam/Leiden 1996.

Beukers, H., *The mission of Hippocrates in Japan. The contribution of Philipp Franz von Siebold.* Amsterdam 1998.

Boxer, C.R., *Zeevarend Nederland en zijn wereldrijk 1600-1800.* Leiden 1976.

Forrer, M., 'The Leiden-collections of Philipp Franz von Siebold', in: *Die Japansammlungen Philipp Franz und Heinrich von Siebolds.* (Miscellanea, 12, 1996). Tokyo, Deutsches Institut für Japanstudien.

Forrer, M., 'Warera no Deshima: Orandajin ni yoru rekishiteki kōsatsu', in: *Deshima Oranda shōkan fukugen o mezashite (Dai ikkai Nichiran kōryū 400-nen kinen kokusai shinposhium kiroku)* Nagasaki 1998, pp. 39-68.

Gids der Japansche tentoonstelling. National Museum of Ethnology. Haarlem 1899.

Goodman, K. Grant, *Japan. The Dutch experience.* London 1986.

Gulik, W.R. van, *Nederlanders in Nagasaki - Japanse prenten uit de 19e eeuw / The Dutch in Nagasaki - 19th-century Japanese prints.* Amsterdam 1998.

Gulik, W.R. van, 'Von Siebold and his Japanese collection in Leiden', in: W. Otterspeer (ed.), *Leiden Oriental connections 1850-1940.* Leiden/New York etc., 1989, pp. 378-91.

In het spoor van de Liefde. Japans-Nederlandse ontmoetingen sinds 1600. Amsterdam 1986.

Hamy, E-T., *Les origines du Musée d'Ethnographie.* Paris 1988.

Holthuis, L.B. & T. Sakai, *Ph.F. von Siebold and Fauna Japonica. A history of early Japanese zoology.* Tokyo 1970.

Ishiyama Yoshikazu, *Shiiboruto no Nihon kenkyū.* Tokyo: Yoshikawa Kōbunkan, 1997.

Körner, H. 'Siebold. Beiträge zur Familiengeschichte', in: *Die Würzbürger Siebold. Eine Gelehrtenfamilie des 18. und 19. Jahrhunderts.* (Deutsches Familienarchiv. Ein genealogisches Sammelwerk, Band 34/35). Neustadt a/d Aisch 1967, pp. 356-491.

Kreiner, J. (ed.), *Shiiboruto fushi no mita Nihon. Seitan 200-nen kinen.* Tokyo: Deutsches Institut für Japanstudien, 1996.

Kreiner, J. (ed.), *Tasogare no Tokugawa Japan. Shiiboruto fushi no mita Nihon*. Tokyo: NHK Books, 842, 1998.

Kure Shūzō, *Shiiboruto sensei: Sono seigai oyobi kōgyō*. Tokyo: Tohōdō shoten, 1926.

Kure Shūzō, *Philipp Franz von Siebold Leben und Werk*. Bearbeitet von Friedrich M. Trautz. Monographien aus dem Deutschen Institut für Japanstudien der Philipp-Franz-von-Siebold-Stiftung; Bd. 17/1,2. München 1996.

Kure Shūzō, 'Ph. Fr. v. Siebold und sein Einfluss auf die japanische Zivilisation der neueren Zeit', in: *Feestbundel uitgegeven door het Koninklijk Bataviaasch Genootschap van Kunsten en Wetenschappen bij gelegeheid van zijn 150 jarig bestaan, 1778-1928*. Weltevreden: G. Kolff & Co., 1929, pp. 410-29.

Leemans, C. *Korte handleiding bij het bezigtigen van het Rijks Japansch Museum von Siebold*. Leiden 1860.

MacLean, J. 'The enrichment of the Royal Cabinet of Rarities at 's-Gravenhage with Japanese ethnographical specimens from 1815 to 1848', in: *Japanese studies in the history of science*, 14 (1975). Tokyo: The History of Science Society of Japan, pp. 117-39.

Manners and customs of the Japanese in the nineteenth century. From the accounts of Dutch residents in Japan and from the German work of Dr. Philipp Franz von Siebold. Rutland, Vermont & Tokyo 1973.

Miyazaki Michio, *Shiiboruto to sakoku - kaikoku Nihon*. Kyoto: Shibunkaku shuppan, 1997.

Miyazaki Michio (ed), *Nihon shisōshi, 55: Tokushū Shiiboruto*. Tokyo: Perikansha, 1999.

Nagasaki-Deshimaten. Tokyo: Shōgakukan, 1986.

Nippon. Archiv zur Beschreibung von Japan und dessen Neben- und Schutzländern Jezo miṭ den süd-lichen Kurilen, Sachalin, Korea und den Liukiu Inseln von Ph.Fr. von Siebold herausgegeben von sei-nen Söhnen. Würzburg und Leipzig, 1897.

Noever, P. *et al.*, *Das alte Japan. Spuren und Objekte der Siebold-Reisen*. München/New York 1997.

Philipp Franz von Siebold. A contribution to the study of historical relations between Japan and the Netherlands. Leiden 1978.

Philipp Franz von Siebold (1796-1866). Ein Bayer als Mittler zwischen Japan und Europa. München 1993.

[Rassers, W.H.], *Overzicht van de geschiedenis van het Rijksmuseum voor Volkenkunde, 1837- 1937. Gedenkschrift uitgegeven bij de heropening van het museum op den 30sten November 1937.* Leiden, s.a. [1937].

Red-hair medicine. Dutch-Japanese medical relations. Amsterdam 1991.

Sansom, G.B., *The Western world and Japan.* New York 1950.

Siebold, Alexander Freiherr von, *Ph.Fr. von Siebold's letzte Reise nach Japan, 1859-1862.* Berlin 1903.

Sirks, M.J., *Indisch natuuronderzoek. Een beknopte geschiedenis van de beoefening der natuurwetenschappen in de Nederlandsche koloniën.* Amsterdam, 1915.

Tjon Sie Fat, L.A., *Flora Japonica, Fauna Japonica.* Leiden 1987.

Tjon Sie Fat, L.A. en G.J.C.N. van Vliet, *Philipp von Siebold. Zijn Japanse flora en fauna.* Haarlem 1990.

Viallé, C.R.M.K.L., *Miseraties. De lakwerken in de verzamelingen van J. Cock Blomhoff, J.F. van Overmeer Fisscher en P.F. von Siebold,* [...]. Amsterdam 1984 (unpublished dissertation).

Vos, K., *Assignment Japan. Von Siebold pioneer and collector.* Leiden 1989.

Yamaguchi Takao, 'Von Siebold and Japanese botany', in: *Calanus,* Special number 1: 11-238, 1997.

Yamaguchi, Takao and Nobushige Kato, 'The material of the species dealt in von Siebold's Flora Japonica I', in: *Calanus,* Special number II: 1-21, 52-441, 1998.

Yōroppa ni nemuru Nihon no takara - Shiiboruto korekushon. (Nagasaki Prefectural Art Museum), Tokyo: Bungeishunju, 1990.